The New Indoor Plant Book

the NEW INDOOR PLANT *book*

JOHN EVANS

Photographs by Jacqui Hurst
Illustrations by Sally Maltby

KYLE CATHIE LIMITED

First published in Great Britain in 1993 by
Kyle Cathie Limited
7/8 Hatherley Street, London SW1P 2QT

Paperback edition published 1994

ISBN 1 85626 152 2

A Cataloguing in Publication record for this title is
available from the British Library.

Designed by Geoff Hayes

Printed and bound in Hong Kong
Produced by Mandarin Offset

Contents

Introduction

I have been involved with the growing and selling of pot plants all my life. The family business started back in 1876 in south London, moving to Sidcup in the early 1900s and to Ruxley in 1960. We had stands in Covent Garden Market for more than one hundred years, where our plants were sold to the London florists.

In the old days, before my time, the pot plants, loose on shelves, were loaded on to covered carts. Then in the evening driver, horse and cart would slowly wend their way to market. There the plants would be unloaded with the help of porters and set up individually on our stands, ready for my grandfather and his brother to sell them the next morning. I understand there was many a time when the horse found his own way back to the nursery with the driver snoring heavily as a result of a few too many at one of the multitude of ale houses which abounded in the Covent Garden area.

Now we have insulated temperature-controlled vehicles with air suspension. The plants are boxed, care carded, pre-priced, barcoded, sleeved, in fact given state of the art treatment to ensure that they are in peak condition when they reach the retailers' shelves.

Over the last twenty-five years a complete metamorphosis has taken place throughout the indoor plant industry due to a more affluent society, a change in retailing patterns and greatly improved distribution methods. Many books have been written on houseplants, and women's magazines, newspapers and periodicals all have articles on the multitude of species and varieties, which has helped both to popularize plants enormously and to dispel the mystique surrounding the care of plants.

Once upon a time, plants could be bought only at a florist's or at your local nursery. From America in the 1960s came the concept of garden centres. These sprang up in every part of the country and our own at Ruxley Manor was one of the first. Among the many items for sale were houseplants, standing on benches in glasshouse conditions. Never before had plants been sold from conditions similar to those in which they had grown.

Pot plant sales literally took off. From a once fairly limited range available, growers began to seek new plants from Europe and further afield to provide more choice for the customer in the home. The multiples saw their opportunity and Marks and Spencer were the first to sell pot plants in volume in the United Kingdom. But additional demands were then made upon the growers.

RIGHT: *Hedera helix* (ivy) in its variegated form and *Ficus benjamina* (Weeping fig) are two of the most common and versatile indoor plants, easy to grow and long-lasting. Here they are combined with a *begonia rex* and a cyclamen.

Gone were the days of a plant is a plant is a plant. Rigid specifications were placed on every pot: the height, the width, the degree of openness of the flowers, the colour range, the variety to be grown, the hardening off period – all so that the customer would get the best out of the plant once purchased.

This really set the trend for the future of the industry. Allied to the breeding of new varieties, the specialist growers, seed houses and research stations both here and abroad are placing more emphasis on providing plants that will keep better and be more able to cope with the change in conditions from the glasshouse to the home.

Today the glasshouse that produces houseplants is a highly sophisticated place, with computers controlling the heating, watering, lighting and ventilation to very fine limits, so that the plants are able to enjoy near natural conditions. Once in the home, conditions can be very different, but this the grower knows and so makes every effort to acclimatize the plants before they leave the nursery. The industry and the public alike have much to thank Marks and Spencer for.

Today, along with the garden centres, flower shops and market stalls, most multiples the world over sell indoor plants and more people than ever are enjoying the beauty, both in colour and foliage, that plants can bring to the home.

At home, experimentation is vital. How much time are you prepared to devote to caring for your plants? Are you prepared to learn from mistakes? And try again? I was asked to write this book because my editor had failed three times with the same plant, an extremely beautiful new indoor plant adapted from a cut flower. Acknowledging your contribution will direct you into either choosing plants labelled as easy in this book or into tackling the more challenging ones.

The range of pot plants I have chosen should be widely available, as all are grown commercially, though some may only be stocked by the larger garden centres.

Also, I have tried to provide a wide range of foliage plants in varying hues and leaf types, and flowering ones that will follow the seasons covering a wide colour band. After all, plants are like people – different shapes, sizes and colours. And, like people, they all have their aches and pains. Yet they are very adaptable and resilient, though, of course, some are more so than others. There are detailed care instructions about every plant in this book, but basically all that is needed is common sense and consideration for the plant's natural preferences.

Large plants, small plants, hanging plants, and specimen plants – they all have their place, providing the warmth, colour and sheer magic that only they can give.

Easy Care
A long term houseplant which in good conditions will last many years. **Light** — *Bright natural light is best, direct sunlight may scorch leaves, in shade the plant will become spindly. The plant will grow towards the light, turn it occasionally to maintain its shape. Keep away from cold winter draughts.* **Water** — *Water only when the compost is almost dry. Overwatering or standing the pot in water will suffocate the roots and cause the plant to die.* **Feed** — *Weekly April - September with a houseplant fertiliser.* **Other Information** — *Keep leaves dust free, by wiping with a damp cloth, Leafshine can be used on this plant.* **Do not place this container on a polished surface as scratching or staining may occur.**

MARKS & SPENCER PLC
BAKER STREET
LONDON
© 1992

G200

Most plants sold today have care cards giving instructions on how to look after the plant. These instructions range from being thoroughly vague to pertinently precise. Overall the standard has improved greatly and the major multiples and garden centres have gone to great lengths to provide concise information. I have chose the Marks and Spencer 'Easy Care' range as a benchmark.

The care card is split into seven sections, designed to suit all the plants the store sells, and the instructions are really as good as one will ever get on such a small piece of plastic!

An expression such as 'bright natural light, but keep out of direct sun' advises you to keep the plant in a bright area but away from the direct rays of the sun that may come through a window. 'Water only when the compost is almost dry' means water when the compost on the top has dried out.

A specimen plant can be used to great effect in this striking black Victorian fireplace. The blue *Hydrangea* will do fine away from the light it would get near the window for 2 or 3 weeks but should then be moved to a lighter position for the balance of its flowering period

Indoor plants in the home

Plants bring a home to life!

They have the most amazing range of colours – *natural* colours that can add a great deal even to the most beautifully decorated room. The indoor plant can be used as the focal point in an otherwise functional room or it can provide interest in a dull corner. It can bring colour to the view from a window or be used against a busy wallpaper to produce a sense of calm. And many together can create a dramatic effect, such as foliage plants conjuring up a jungle look. In fact there are so many opportunities for plants indoors – provided, of course, you can offer the conditions in which the plant will thrive.

Large plants will almost always have more dramatic effect if on their own and can even take the place of a piece of furniture. Some of the smaller plants make a better impression when grouped together within the room, the combination of colours adding to their 'noticeability'. In either case there should be sufficient space for the plants to grow and develop.

Natural clay and terracotta pots show off indoor plants particularly well, as do white china ones. There are many patterned china pots to choose from, too, and it is simply a matter of matching the colours of leaf or flower to those of the pot. Wicker or bamboo baskets make attractive alternatives but ensure they are lined to prevent water from seeping through on to the floor or furniture. Ethnic shops often sell beautiful pots which, though perhaps not originally intended for plants, can be adapted to effective use.

And don't forget that you can create interesting designs by displaying plants on glass shelves and against mirrors. The reflection also provides increased light, which is beneficial if light levels are low.

The following pages contain design ideas for plants in some of the less ideal spots in a flat or house. Obviously these are only suggestions and there are many other possibilities – but remember, it is important to match the conditions in which you expect a plant to grow with those the plant requires in order to stay at its best.

The bathroom

Some bathrooms are heated throughout the winter, while others have no source of heat at all – both types of room have a range of plants that will thrive in them. Indeed, the bathroom is one of the best rooms for an indoor plant (provided there is sufficient light and heat) because there are few plants that don't welcome the humidity generated by the warm bath water.

If the window is small and the glass opaque there may be a problem with light. Choose plants that don't mind minimal light, such as *Philodendron scandens* (the sweetheart plant), *Davallia* (the rabbit's foot fern), or *Epipremnum*. *Philodendron scandens* and *Epipremnum* will grow easily as climbers or trailing plants, quickly transforming the starkness of bathroom surfaces. *Adiantum* and *Begonia* are more delicate but like moist air, warmth and shade. They should be removed from the bathroom in winter.

Bathrooms with large windowsills are a joy and many of the ferns and palms will welcome these conditions. I particularly recommend *Syngonium* 'White Butterfly', *Chrysalidocarpus lutescens*, asparagus, *Pellionia*, *Peperomia* and both *Maranta leuconeura* and *Maranta tricolor*. It is often possible to fit an indoor plant into the corner of a bath surround, and all too frequently this is a fairly dark spot where *Aglaonema* (Chinese evergreen) or *Chlorophytum* (spider plant) would do well. *Tolmiea menziesii* (piggyback plant), with its pretty speckled leaves, is compact and well suited to an unheated bathroom though more demanding of light. It can also be grown in a hanging basket above the bath, as can the members of the *Nephrolepsis* fern family, the most popular varieties being 'Boston' and 'Teddy Junior', though 'Linda' which has a more delicate feathery appearance is worth looking out for.

Again introduce flowering plants to provide a kaleidoscope of colour throughout the year. *Saintpaulia* (the African violet) and *Streptocarpus* (the Cape primrose) will flower right through the summer. The humidity and warmth of the bathroom heightens the perfume of fragrant flowers. The first plant to kick off the New Year with would be the winter-flowering jasmine followed by the gardenia, then *Stephanotis* (the Madagascar jasmine) or *Exacum* (the Arabian violet) or *Hoya bella* with its beautiful porcelain-like flowers.

Once flowering is over, remove the plants from the bathroom and allow them to grow under better light conditions elsewhere in the house, or better still in the conservatory or greenhouse.

Here *Adiantum* (the maidenhair fern) thrives on the moisture from the bathroom, not minding the lack of light. The delicate *Streptocarpus* complements the shape of the fern fronds.

Dark hallways and corridors

Entrance halls often lack light and can be very draughty, with doors opening off in various directions. Temperatures at night may be cold, if there is any heating at all. So tough, shade-loving plants are required long term, with flowering plants used as short-term disposable items to provide dramatic focal points of colour among the more sombre green foliage. Together these plants will bring life and vibrancy to what could otherwise be a fairly soulless area of the home.

In looking for a long-term resident for dark corridors, choose a Swiss cheese plant (*Monsteria deliciosa*) or the smaller leaved *Philodendron pertusum.* You could also try, from the same family, the *Philodendron scandens* and *Philodendron selloum* or the *Fatshedera lizei* (tree ivy) with its rich glossy leaves. These can all be table plants, but are also ideal as feature plants, growing up moss poles to heights of around 2m/4–5ft – real sentries in the corridor.

The aspidistra, or cast-iron plant, is practically indestructible and is presently enjoying a new wave of popularity. Then there is *Aglaonema* (the Chinese evergreen), *Rhoicissus rhomboidea* (the grape ivy), and not forgetting the *Platycerium* (staghorn fern). You will find you have a plethora of plants to choose from.

Now for some flowering plants to add that spot of dash and brilliance – how about a basket of cyclamen or azaleas, a large azalea on its own, a container of chrysanthemums, a single hydrangea or the beautiful slipper orchid (*Paphiopedilum*) or moth orchid (*Phalaenopsis*). Again, choose the plant to fit the season, displayed either on its own or massed together with others according to the size of the hall or space.

For a plant that enjoys longevity as a foliage plant yet also produces a flower, you cannot beat the *Spathiphyllum* (white sails).

Use simple single foliage plants to maximize drama in a bland dark passageway. These will give more pleasure than a collection of straggly plants growing desperately towards whatever small light source there may be.

Always rotate the plants to which you give difficult conditions. A spell of two to three months in a more sympathetic situation will do much to restore their vigour.

ABOVE: A single plant – in this case a delicate pink *Primula malacoides* (fairy primrose) – can bring life to a dark corner.

RIGHT: *Nephrolepsis* (sword fern) does sterling work, here combined with *Spathiphyllum* (white sails) to provide interest in a dark hallway. On the shelf to the right is the indispensable *Scindapsus* (devil's ivy) and on the stairs the aspidistra complements two yuccas.

Conservatories and garden rooms

Many of us dream of having a room we can devote to a collection of rich, green, sweet-scented plants, and since the 1970s there has been a vast increase in the number of conservatories built. There are certain advantages in having a conservatory – chiefly that the light reaches the plants from all sides, similar both to the environment of their native habitat and to that in which they are raised in the commercial greenhouse. Also, today's conservatories often have proper ventilation systems to keep the air fresh and blinds to shade delicate plants from the midday sun, preventing scorched leaves.

Decide on the purpose of your conservatory – is it a formal dining room or a casual extension to the sitting room, a plant room where a jungle fantasy can be indulged or simply a hideaway? – and choose plants that complement that purpose. Having a conservatory is a luxury, but at the same time it requires a commitment of time and energy.

When choosing the plants, look for some of the exotic species that can't commonly be grown around the house. This will, of course, depend to some extent on the amount of heat you can provide in the cooler months of the year, but there is a very wide range of plants that can be grown in a room with a winter temperature of only 10–13°C/50–55°F. Also make sure that you have a supply of water within easy access of the conservatory as there will be a great deal of watering to be done.

A comfortable garden room making good use of sweet-scented *Citris mitis* and *Mimosa*

Some of the more exotic species that can be tried include *Agapanthus* (try *A. campanulatus*, a vigorous, blue variety which happily adapts to sun-room conditions); *Citrus*, with its beautifully scented white flowers and pretty small orange fruits; or some of the rarer orchids: try the vibrant pink *Cattleya bowringiana. Laelia purpurata* is the national flower of Brazil and can be brought into flower in late winter or early spring; it is not difficult for the beginner. The *Abutilon, Bougainvillea, Columnea, Gloriosa* and *Oleander* are other exotics well worth trying.

The jungle aspect of a conservatory is created by the foliage plants. Look to the palm family, and here I recommend *Howea* (the kentia palm) and *Chrysalidocarpus lutescens* (the areca palm). *Rhapis excelsa* (the lady palm), a relatively new addition to the commercial range, is worth looking out for. All the *Ficus* varieties do well, and of course I recommend *Ficus benjamina*, either variegated or plain green. *Ficus lyrata*, with its rich big leaves, can also create a strong impact. *Philodendron* is tailer-made for the conservatory, whether trailing or growing up a moss pole. Another good architectural plant is *Dracaena marginata,* which will provide stark contrasts with its whitish stem and spiky foliage.

Remember that the conditions in a conservatory will suit plants with variegated or coloured leaves, the light bringing up the intensity of their leaf patterns; so try to include *Codiaeum, Cordyline terminalis, Caladium, Dieffenbachia exotica, Hibiscus, Maranta* and some of the *Begonia rex* cultivars.

Terracotta pots are particularly effective in conservatories and garden rooms. Here, sweet scented geraniums are used to good effect; also the bold leaves of avocado are complimented by the purple flowers of *Bougainvillea*, which is happy only with plenty of light

Windowsills

At first sight the windowsill seems the ideal place for plants, but there can still be problems.

Sunny windowsills

Here there is a danger of the leaves being burned by the sun and of the plants drying out very quickly, particulary in summer. Where the windowsill takes the full face of the midday sun, a protective screen such as very light curtaining is well worth considering. There are few plants able to withstand such hot situations, the exceptions being *Coleus*, *Bougainvillea*, *Sansevieria*, *Beaucarnea* and *Yucca*, but these all need to be kept well watered. The *Echeveria*, coming from the dry Mexican plateau, can also hold its own in the midday sun.

Consider the conditions of a sunny windowsill in winter. In the evening the curtains are drawn, the radiators go off during the night and the plant is subjected to dramatically changing temperatures, so it is always best to bring the plant into the body of the room before closing the curtains.

However, as the sun is weak during winter a much larger range of plants can be displayed.

Windowsills with little or no sun

This location opens the doors for a wide range of plants.

Many of the foliage plants such as *Chlorophytum* (spider plant), the aspidistra, the *Dracaena* family, the *Schefflera*, *Aglaonema* and the *Philodendron* family will grow quite healthily in indirect light conditions.

Again flowering plants should be used to provide colour and then removed after flowering.

Where curtains and radiators are involved during the winter, move the plants into the room at night.

On this windowsill display a *Yucca*, *Sansevieria* and *Beaucarnea* are combined with two examples of *Soleirolia soleirolii*. During winter nights, when the curtains are closed and the radiators turned off, these plants should ideally be removed from the sill

Dry atmosphere plants

Plants need humidity, but there are a few plants that will do well in centrally heated rooms with little ventilation. The most obvious group of these plants is the cacti family as they are long-living and can put up with neglect. They are also plants which people seem to either love or loathe.

There are two groups in this family – the desert cacti and the forest cacti. Both originate from Central America, the former, and by far the larger group, growing in semi-desert regions; the latter growing on trees as epiphytes in the woodlands and jungles.

Of the foliage plants, *Phoenix canariensis, Yucca* and *Beaucarnea* will thrive in a dry atmosphere as will *Aloe* and *Brachychiton*. The *Eustoma* will bloom happily, as will *Bougainvillea, Hibiscus* and *Kalanchoe*, and the regal and zonal pelargoniums.

Plants will almost always be improved if placed on pebble trays, particularly those situated near a radiator. Look, too, at species which can tolerate room temperatures throughout the year and do not require cool winter conditions for the dormant season.

Consider what function you want your plants to fulfil. Dramatic branch shapes such as those of the *Dracaena marginata* can make a sparsely furnished room – either a living room or dining room – more 'furnished'. A group of palms can act as a divider between living and eating areas (but remember there must be enough room so that you don't constantly knock the plants). Alternatively, small plants could be used as centrepieces on dining-room tables, on side boards or on shelving. A simple arrangement of *Soleirolia soleirolii* (mind your own business), for example, can make the most effective table decoration.

Plants act as humidifiers of dry, centrally-heated air. They make the rooms healthier to live in and even produce minimal amounts of oxygen. However, they also filter out dust, which will settle on the leaves and should be wiped off from time to time.

The recommended humidity level for most houseplants is between 60–70 per cent but in many rooms the humidity falls to around 35 per cent. In the dry atmosphere room humidity can be improved with an electric humidifier, which will also help to protect antique furniture from the effects of central heating.

OPPOSITE: Three plants that can tolerate the dry atmosphere of a centrally heated room: *Bougainvillea* (at the back), *Kalanchoe* (on the right) and *Hibiscus* (at the front). All grow naturally in hot climates where rainfall is light during the summer months

Winter colour

Fortunately, when there are limited supplies of cut flowers from the garden there are plenty of colourful indoor flowering plants to bring cheer to a dull winter's day. Among the most obvious are the poinsettia – we sell over 8 acres of these in their red, orangy-pink and cream varieties through autumn up to Christmas. With good treatment these should keep their coloured bracts for three to four months.

Azalea indica flowers for up to a month during the winter and makes an excellent houseplant. Treat yourself to a miniature standard at Christmas. The versatile *Saintpaulia* (African violet) flowers happily in winter months, as do the primroses, *Primula obconica*, *Primula malacoides* and *Primula acaulis*, each producing a brilliant range of colours.

One of the most commonly sold pot plants is *Cyclamen*, as it is able to tolerate quite cold conditions. It is often seen in window boxes and can withstand a slight frost though a severe one can prove fatal. *Clivia* comes into flower in the late winter months, with its bold orange flower heads strikingly contrasted against the deep green of the leaves. *Kalanchoe* is another plant that flowers freely and lasts well, particularly on a kitchen windowsill. With the advent of special growing lamps in commercial nurseries *Begonia elatior* and *Campanula*, not withstanding the ever-popular *Chrysanthemum indicum* hybrids (the pot chrysanthemums), are freely available. The red 'sails' of *Anthurium* look seasonally cheerful during the winter months and can do much to enliven a dark corner. This plant can also be arranged with the white *Spathiphyllum* to make a highly decorative Christmas display.

Many of the plants you buy at this time of year will have been forced into flower by nursery men. When we force plants into flower we normally have a predetermined date in mind. For example, we know that certain *Azalea* varieties flower around December but to ensure they are ready in the two-week run up to Christmas and not one week late or two weeks early, one has to pay particular attention to detail. Mistakes still occur, but computerization and sophisticated controls, together with the skill of the grower, have helped ensure that the plants arrive in the shops in mint condition.

OPPOSITE: The exotic bright red flowers of *Anthurium* can bloom throughout the year and are set off beautifully by the glossy heart-shaped leaves. Here it is paired with the pot chrysanthemum, which has also been bred to be available in flower all year round

Here *Begonia elatior* provides a splash of winter colour

Foliage Plants

There is a rich variety of foliage plants to choose from when decorating your house. The leaf forms and patterns are endless, as this is where photosynthesis and respiration are carried out. On the one hand, there is the enchanting pink and cream colour bands on the delicate green leaves of the *Hypoestes* or the *Tradescantia*, on the other the strongly patterned veins of the *Fittonia* or the *Croton*.

There are plants with delicate and graceful fronds, plants that trail and climb, plants that will reach to the ceiling, plants that will form screens – practically an infinite range.

Whilst the plants in this book are divided into foliage and flowering groups, these divisions are artificial as in the main the foliage plants do flower.

The range of foliage plants marketed has grown vastly since the 1950s, and this book aims to include some of the newer varieties you should look out for.

Acalypha hispida (Chenille plant, red hot cattail)

DIFFICULT

A native of the tropical jungle forests of Java and Papua New Guinea, this tall ornamental shrub has bright green oval leaves with hairy undersides. In spring and summer it produces long pendant spikes of bright red flowers that should be removed when they are past their best. The plant can be pruned at the same time.

Acalypha hispida is a quick grower and needs the warm, humid temperatures of its native habitat all year round. Stand the pot over damp gravel or pack it with moist peat and spray every day, avoiding the flowers when they are blooming. It is quite difficult to maintain its humidity requirements in autumn and winter, so if possible put it in a greenhouse or conservatory at this time.

As a houseplant it will grow up to 2m/6ft, but it is advisable to propagate each year from stem cuttings.

Also available is *Acalypha wilksiana*, which has attractive coppery-red leaves, hence its common name 'copperleaf'.

Acalypha hispida

A. hispida 'Balik'

A. wilksiana 'Can Can'

A. wilksiana hybrid 'Harlequin'

CARE

Light and temperature
Bright but indirect light and a constant warm temperature all year, no higher than 26°C/80°F in summer and no lower than 16°C/61°F in winter.

Water and feeding
Water thoroughly in spring and summer, but do not allow the plant to stand in water or the soil to become soggy. Spray the foliage frequently until the flowers start to form, then place the pot over a saucer of pebbles almost covered with water to provide good humidity. Do not spray while in flower. Feed fortnightly with a general liquid fertilizer until after flowering.

Propagation
By 7.5–10cm/3–4in stem cuttings, which should be dusted with rooting powder and established in sandy soil under a plastic cover at a constant temperature of 23°C/75°F.

Repotting
Cut the plant back in early spring to 25cm/10in above a leaf and repot into a 13cm/5in pot using a no. 2 soil-based compost with good drainage.

PROBLEMS

White woolly patches on the stems and leaves indicate mealy bug. Remove with a cloth dipped in methylated spirit.

Webs on the underside of leaves indicate red spider mite. Spray with a systemic insecticide and check humidity level.

Adiantum (Maidenhair fern)

Adiantum fragrans

QUITE EASY

This most delicate of ferns, with dainty, fan like, pale green triangular leaves on black wiry stalks, comes from the tropical and subtropical areas of Australia, New Zealand and the Americas, where it is to be found growing amongst rocks. Some hardy or nearly hardy varieties grow in the United Kingdom.

It is not difficult to grow indoors, but requires constant monitoring to ensure it does not dry out. This plant needs a steady, humid atmosphere with no direct sunlight, and does well in bathrooms and the shaded parts of a conservatory or greenhouse. Keep the roots moist, but not wet, and spray often, daily if in a heated room.

Adiantum will grow to 60cm/24in across and 30–38cm/12–15in high. There are some 200 varieties, but the most common ones available are *monocolor*, *fragrans*, *scuteum roseum* and 'Fritz Lutzii'.

It is a very long-lasting plant.

A. scuteum roseum

'Fritz Lutzii'

A. monocolor

CARE

Light and temperature
Adiantum grows well in warm, humid and sheltered spots away from direct sunlight. It dislikes both draughts and dry air. The minimum winter temperature is 10°C/50°F and the maximum summer temperature 24°C/75°F.

Water and feeding
The roots must not be allowed to dry out. It is best to submerge the pot in water for 10 minutes, then drain, probably twice weekly in summer and once a week in winter. Feed fortnightly with liquid fertilizer from mid-spring to mid-autumn or use slow-release pellets. These plants love a high degree of humidity in warm temperatures. Spray leaves daily and stand the container on moist pebbles.

Propagation
In spring divide the clumps, leaving a piece of rhizome attached to each clump, and place in a good peat-based compost to which you have added a little fertilizer.

Repotting
Repot in a peat-based compost each spring. Pack the soil lightly as good drainage is essential.

PROBLEMS

Most problems arise from a lack of moisture and humidity.

If the fronds dry up, cut them off and spray daily until new shoots appear.

If the leaves drop, the plant can be cut right back to encourage new growth. Continue watering and spraying while it becomes established.

If the leaves turn pale, the plant has received too much sunlight. Move it out of the sun and into a shadier position.

Aglaonema (Chinese evergreen)

EASY

This group of plants was discovered in the nineteenth century in China and the tropical rainforests and islands of Malaya, Sri Lanka and the Philippines, where they are to be found growing in the shady spots under the tree canopy. There are quite a few varieties, which make good houseplants if kept at a constant temperature and humidity, away from draughts, fires or heaters. They present few problems apart from the occasional yellow leaf if underfed in summer or if allowed to get too cold in winter.

Aglaonema commutatum has decorative variegated foliage – large spear-shaped leaves with silver-green stripes or dots. Sometimes they bloom and, after flowering, develop poisonous red berries.

The plant grows to about 25cm/10in tall and will produce 5–6 new leaves a year. *Aglaonema roebelenii* has thick, leathery, grey-green leaves which grow up to 30cm/1ft long. *Aglaonema crispum* has dark green and silver leaves. The all-green varieties do not require much light, but those with white or variegated yellow foliage need brighter conditions.

The plant will slow down after 2–3 years and should be started again with stem-tip cuttings.

A. roebelenii or
A. crispum
(painted drop tongue)

CARE

Light and temperature
It grows well in constant conditions, without much light, and is fairly tolerant of low temperatures. Ideally temperatures are between 15–24°C/60–75°F – it will withstand 10°C/50°F, but keep the plant on the dry side if the temperature drops this low.

Water and feeding
In summer water thoroughly twice weekly and add liquid fertilizer every 14 days. Do not allow to dry out. Keep much drier in winter. It likes humidity in summer and benefits from spraying twice weekly or being placed over a saucer of wet pebbles. The plant does well in hydroculture.

Propagation
The easiest way to propagate is by division of the root clump. The plant should then be established in a propagator as it will need a high humidity.

Repotting
Repot only as needed, in spring, in a good open compost as the roots like to breathe and good drainage is important.

PROBLEMS

Mealy bug can be a problem, as can red spider mite, if conditions are too light and too dry. Remove them with a cloth soaked in methylated spirit or spray with a systemic insecticide.

Aglaonema commutatum is commonly known as the silver evergreen

Aloe vera (Medicine plant, Barbados aloe, true aloe)

EASY

Aloe vera is sometimes known as *A. barbadensis*

CARE

Light and temperature
Aloe thrives in direct sunlight and a warm temperature, ideally 18°C/64°F. In winter ensure it continues to receive full sunlight and temperatures no lower than 8°C/47°F.

Water and feeding
Immerse the pot in water for 10 minutes, drain well, and allow the compost almost to dry out between waterings. Take care not to let the water settle in the rosette. In winter it will need watering only every 3–4 weeks. Feed monthly in spring and summer with a liquid solution.

Propagation
In spring by removing lateral shoots. The plant yields a sticky pap, so the shoot should be left to dry for 2 days before being planted in a just-damp mixture of no. 2 compost and sand. It should root easily at normal room temperature.

Repotting
Repot young plants annually in spring in a no. 2 potting compost.

PROBLEMS

Take care not to overwater this plant or to let water settle in the rosette as this will cause stem rot, which is recognizable by black marks on the leaves. Allow the compost to dry out completely before watering again and check that the temperature is not too cold.

If the leaves turn brown and dry, the plant has been kept too dry. Soak thoroughly in water for 1 hour and then drain.

If the leaves are a poor colour, the plant does not have enough light. Move to a brighter position.

Aloe vera may be attacked by scale insect. Spray with a systemic insecticide.

This medicinal member of the lily family is a very popular houseplant. Its juice is said to have healing properties for burns, skin and hair, hence its name.

Originally from the semi-arid, subtropical islands of Cape Verde, Canary and Madeira, it is hardy and virtually problem-free. It likes a sunny spot with dry air, the same conditions it enjoys in its native habitat.

Aloe vera grows as a rosette of fleshy, stiff, pointed, grey-green, spotted leaves. It may produce yellow flowers. It is a long-lasting plant and will benefit from a spell outdoors in a sunny, protected spot. There are many new species being marketed.

Ampelopsis (Chinese grape)

EASY

This charming hanging plant resembles a grapevine in the way it trails attractively over a pot or basket. It produces a profusion of long red stems from which grow white or pink marbled leaves.

Originally from the eastern areas of China, *Ampelopsis* grows naturally in the warm temperate rainforests, wrapping itself around the branches and trunks of trees.

It is a good houseplant, easy to look after and a quick grower. It will thrive in both bright and semi-shady conditions as long as it has a reasonable amount of humidity in the form of misting; a conservatory is an ideal spot to grow this plant. It will also benefit from a spell outside in summer.

The plant has a dormant period in winter. It will lose its leaves in late autumn, after which it should be pruned. It can then be reshaped in spring if necessary. Pinch out the new growing tips if you would like a denser plant.

It should live for several years. When the plant is past its best it can be propagated.

Ampelopsis brevipedunculata should be kept in a light position with enough heat to retain its lovely pink-marbled leaves

CARE

Light and temperature
Enjoys indirect sunlight to semi-shady spots in summer with temperatures of 16–18°C/60–64°F. Though deciduous, it also likes bright conditions in winter and a temperature of 5–12°C/41–54°F.

Water and feeding
During spring and summer water thoroughly and do not let the plant dry out. Feed fortnightly with general houseplant fertilizer to manufacturer's recommendations. During winter keep the plant almost dry and prune back hard.

Propagation
From stem-tip cuttings of approximately 10cm/4in in length, making the bottom of the cutting just below a leaf joint with a clean cut. Dip into a rooting hormone and insert it into a peat and sand cutting compost. Water in. Place in a propagator at a temperature of 18°C/64°F.

Repotting
Repot each spring in a no. 2 soil-based compost.

PROBLEMS

Webs on the underside of leaves indicate red spider mite. Spray with a systemic insecticide and keep well watered.

Ananas bracteatus striatus

(Variegated red pineapple)   **EASY**

This spiny-leafed ornamental pineapple is sought after for its spectacular foliage and occasional large brown edible fruits. It forms rosettes of coppery-green pointed leaves which can grow up to 1m/3ft in length, so it needs plenty of space. Always wear gloves when handling it as its leaves are sharp.

Ananas comes from Brazil where it grows naturally and is cultivated in large fields in high temperatures and bright sunlight.

As a houseplant it likes a bright spot but not direct sunlight.

The fruiting spike, usually pink, contrasts attractively with the green and yellow striped leaves. The fruit takes several months to form, usually maturing in spring.

The fruit of the ornamental pineapple needs a lot of space; the rosy-coloured leaves grow up to 1m/40in long and spread as much in width. Dwarf varieties (*Ananas nanus*) are only two-thirds the size.

Ananas bracteatus striatus

CARE

Light and temperature
Ananas requires warm and bright conditions, but not direct sunlight, all year round, with temperatures not below 18°C/64°F in winter. Keep the plant away from cold draughts.

Water and feeding
Water 2-3 times a week in summer and only once a week in winter, allowing the soil to dry out between waterings. Feed every 2 weeks in spring and summer and while the fruit is forming.

Propagation
After fruiting the plant dies down and a small offset grows beside it. When the main plant has begun to shrivel up, separate the offset and its roots with a knife and plant in a 9cm/3.5in pot. Keep moist in a propagator at 20°C/70°F.

Repotting
In spring repot younger plants in a mixture of peat and sand. Older plants will need only the topsoil changed.

PROBLEMS

Ananas is prone to few diseases. It may be attacked by scale insect. Remove these from underneath the leaves with a cloth dipped in methylated spirit.

If the leaves shrivel or the tips are brown, the plant is too dry and hot. Water, spray and move to a cooler position.

If the leaves are a poor colour, move to a brighter spot.

Anthurium scherzerianum

(Flamingo flower)

QUITE DIFFICULT

This plant is grown for its decorative heart-shaped leaves and pretty bright red or white oval flowers with creamy-coloured spadix that grow throughout the year.

Originally from Central and South America, as a houseplant it is fairly small, growing to 25cm/10in with a slightly wider spread.

It is not a quick grower, and is not recommended for the beginner. It will need careful monitoring to make sure the conditions are right and must be kept away from draughts and temperature variations. The soil should never be allowed to dry out and a constant humidity level is essential. Mist frequently and stand the pot over damp gravel.

It should last for several years.

Anthurium scherzerianum has a spadix that is twisted spirally

CARE

Light and temperature
Strong indirect light and a constant temperature of around 18–21°C/64–70°F is ideal. In winter the temperature should not go below 15°C/60°F.

Water and feeding
Water 2–3 times a week in spring and summer, never allowing the compost to dry out. Stand the pot over damp gravel and mist frequently. In winter, it will need less water. In spring and summer fertilize every 2 weeks with a general houseplant solution.

Propagation
Quite difficult. Divide the plant in late winter, ensuring each section has some roots and stems, and plant in a peat-based compost. Establish at a constant temperature of 21°C/70°F.

Repotting
In spring, every second year, in a peat-based compost.

PROBLEMS

This plant can be quite temperamental as it requires the right conditions in order to thrive. If it is too cold and wet or too dry, the leaves will turn yellow. Check the temperature, watering and humidity levels.

Brown spots on the leaves indicate fungus caused by cold and wet conditions. Spray with a systemic fungicide and check temperature and watering.

Prone to mealy bug, red spider mite and aphids. Remove mealy bug and spider mite with a cloth dipped in methylated spirit and spray aphids with a pyrethrum-based insecticide.

Araucaria heterophylla (Norfolk Island pine)

EASY

Discovered in the South Pacific in 1793 by Captain Cook and Sir Joseph Banks, this handsome pine reaches a height of 60m/200ft in its native habitat. As a houseplant it will grow to a much more manageable 1–1.5m/ 3–6ft. It is a slow grower and after reaching this height is past its best.

The Norfolk Island pine is appealing because of its tiered branches covered with pale green needles. Pruning is not recommended, although this will encourage bushier growth if the plant becomes straggly. The lower branches can be cut off when they become bare.

Araucaria requires a bright, well-lit position, and will enjoy a spell outdoors on mild days. It likes freely circulating air, but not central heating. In summer it needs a lot of moisture, so mist frequently.

Indoors it should last for many years. It can also be used as a Christmas tree.

Araucaria heterophylla has stiff needles, resinous sap and can produce cones

CARE

Light and temperature
A bright, well-ventilated position. In summer it likes temperatures between 18–22°C/64–72°F or a semi-shady spot outdoors with a good breeze. In winter it can withstand cooler temperatures of as low as 5°C/40°F.

Water and feeding
Keep the compost moist in spring, summer and autumn. It will need less water in winter. Mist often. Feed in summer at fortnightly intervals with a general houseplant fertilizer.

Propagation
Difficult to propagate from seed. It is better to buy a small established plant.

Repotting
Repot annually in spring until the plant is 1m/3ft tall, then just replace the topsoil.

PROBLEMS

Dry yellow needles mean conditions are too hot and dry. Water and move to a cooler, well-ventilated spot. Mist frequently.

Mealy bug and greenfly can attack this plant. Treat with a pyrethrum-based insecticide.

Aspidistra (Cast-iron plant)

EASY

Aspidistra comes from China, Japan and the Himalayas, where it grows in poor, marshy soil, and tolerates a range of temperatures, bar frost. It has been a popular houseplant since Victorian times because it flourishes in dark and draughty rooms. It is now enjoying revived popularity because it is attractive, easy to look after and able to withstand most conditions.

   A. elatior (also known as *A. lurida*) and *A. elatior* 'Variegata' are the most readily available varieties.

   It is a slow grower, each year producing only a few elegant, arched, shiny dark green leaves of between 30–46cm/12–18in. Occasionally small purple, bell-shaped flowers will appear at soil level.

   Aspidistra will tolerate periods of dryness, but dislikes sunlight, soggy soil and frequent repotting. Clean the leaves with a damp sponge rather than using leaf shine.

   Although it is quite expensive, it is virtually an everlasting houseplant.
It will benefit from a spell outdoors in summer.

Aspidistra elatior

A. elatior 'Variegata' (variegated cast-iron plant)

The yellow or white striped leaves shoot direct from the rhizome

CARE

Light and temperature
A shady position away from bright light or direct sunlight. *Aspidistra* prefers a cool temperature all year of around 13°C/55°F and as low as 7°C/45°F. It will, however, withstand most temperature fluctuations. Variegated species will need a little more light to maintain the leaf colour.

Water and feeding
Immerse the pot in water for 10 minutes and then drain well. Allow the soil almost to dry out between waterings. Never let the plant stand in water. In winter it will need watering less often, especially if the temperature is below 10°C/50°F. Add liquid food monthly and spray occasionally.

Propagation
Divide into small sections in autumn and place in a good potting mixture, ensuring adequate drainage.

Repotting
The plant does not like to be disturbed too often, so repot every 3 or 4 years in a no. 3 compost, ensuring good drainage.

PROBLEMS

If this plant is subjected to sunlight, brown spots will form on the leaves. Move to a shadier position and cut off the damaged leaves.

Aspidistra is susceptible to scale insect, red spider mite and mealy bug. Treat with a systemic insecticide and improve humidity.

Bambusa vulgaris (Bamboo)

EASY

This most exotic-looking houseplant is a relative newcomer. It is grown from a section of bamboo culm which produces a profusion of delicate pale green leafy fronds, giving the appearance of a standard plant.

Bamboo grows freely all over the tropical zones of the Far East, but it has only recently been adapted as a houseplant. It likes bright, sunny conditions and in summer does well outdoors.

A mature plant will grow to about 1m/39in high and the culm is 6–8cm/2–3in in diameter.

It is not particularly long lasting, and will probably have to be replaced after a couple of years.

Bambusa vulgaris

CARE

Light and temperature
This plant likes bright, warm conditions in summer. It will tolerate cooler temperatures in winter, but not below 5°C/40°F.

Water and feeding
Water 2–3 times a week in spring and summer and feed every 3 weeks with a general houseplant fertilizer. Water less in winter, allowing the soil almost to dry out between waterings. Never let the compost get soggy.

Propagation
This plant is difficult to propagate and best left to a professional.

Repotting
This should not be necessary.

PROBLEMS

Bambusa vulgaris is relatively problem free, though it is susceptible to spider mite in winter if the conditions are too warm and dry.

Beaucarnea recurvata (Ponytail plant)

Beaucarnea recurvata

EASY

Originally from the arid desert areas of Mexico, this is a most unusual and eye-catching succulent.

Its bottle-shaped stem serves as a water reservoir and grows several branches from which shoot slim, downward-curving, grey-green leaves of up to 1m/3ft in length. Sometimes it will produce clusters of small white flowers.

As a houseplant it will grow up to 2m/6ft in height and should live for several years.

It likes a bright, sunny position with fresh air and should ideally be positioned near a window. It does not require a lot of attention. Any leaves which fade can be gently peeled off.

Beaucarnea recurvata will benefit from a spell outdoors in summer but must be placed in a protected spot.

CARE

Light and temperature
This plant enjoys bright light and full sun all year round. In winter the temperature should not go below 10°C/50°F.

Water and feeding
Water once a week in summer and less in winter so that the compost stays almost dry. Never let it stand in water. Fertilize with a liquid solution at twice-weekly intervals in summer.

Propagation
By seed or by side shoots in summer. Both will need to be established in greenhouse conditions in a damp compost of peat and sand, covered in plastic and maintained at a temperature of 24°C/75°F.

Repotting
Repot every 2–3 years in a mixture of soil, leaf mould and sand, ensuring good drainage.

PROBLEMS

This plant is relatively problem free as long as it is never left to stand in water.

If its location is too warm and dry it is susceptible to spider mite and scale insect. Treat with a systemic insecticide.

Tips may die back; trim with discretion.

Begonia rex (Leaf begonia)

QUITE EASY

There is an enormous variety of *Begonia rex* hybrids available, and almost all have extremely attractive leaves with beautiful patterns. When choosing, look for good markings and avoid any with damaged leaves or rot on the stem.

Begonia grows in tropical and subtropical areas around the world and specimens from the foothills of the Himalayas were introduced into Europe in Victorian times. It is a most popular houseplant, and will grow to approximately 30cm/12in in height and 46cm/18in in width. It is good as an individual plant or in mixed plantings.

It needs to be kept out of direct sunlight but in a well-lit position and enjoys humidity, but only when the temperature is above 20°C/68°F. It does not like draughts, central heating or varying temperatures.

Begonia leaves are delicate, so treat the plant carefully and do not use leaf shine. Turn the pot regularly to ensure even growth as the plant will tend to grow towards the light.

The plant should last for up to 2 years and is easy to propagate with leaf cuttings.

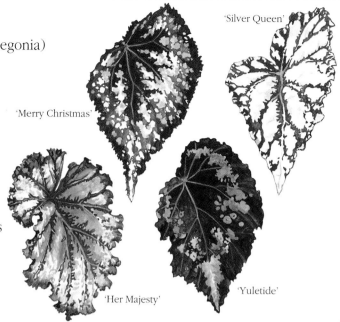

'Silver Queen'

'Merry Christmas'

'Her Majesty'

'Yuletide'

Begonia rex

CARE

Light and temperature
A bright situation but away from direct sunlight. The ideal summer temperature is 21°C/70°F. In winter it can go as low as 10°C/50°F.

Water and feeding
Water twice weekly in summer, with rain water if possible, and spray the leaves regularly. Water only once every 10 days in winter to keep the soil moist. At lower temperatures do not water over the leaves. In spring and summer add liquid fertilizer every 2 weeks.

Propagation
From tip cuttings in late spring. Cut off a shoot below the second pair of leaves. Trim the shoot and remove the lowest pair of leaves. Dip the cut surface in rooting hormone. Insert into compost in a propagator at 21°C/70°F until established.

Repotting
In spring, only when potbound, in a light, open mixture of loam and peat to which a little leaf mould and sand have been added.

PROBLEMS

This is a fragile plant, susceptible to draughts and temperature fluctuations.

If the leaves curl and become brittle, the position is too hot and dry. Water and move to a cooler spot.

If the leaves drop in winter, its position is too cold. Move to a warmer spot.

Red spider mite will cause the leaves to turn dull with webs underneath. Spray with a systemic insecticide.

If there are white or grey powdery patches on the leaves, the plant may have been overwatered and have mildew. Spray with a benomyl-based fungicide and move to a drier area.

Brachychiton rupestris (Queensland bottle tree)

QUITE EASY

This striking plant from Queensland has firm grey-green leaves and a most unusual twisted, bottle-shaped trunk which serves as a water reservoir, necessary in its hot but dry native habitat.

It likes bright, sunny conditions and should spend as much time as possible outdoors. Indoors its ideal location is on a windowsill.

Brachychiton is an undemanding houseplant. It is quite easy to look after and does well in a centrally heated room.

CARE

Light and temperature
In summer *Brachychiton* likes full sun with temperatures between 18–20°C/64–68°F. In winter the temperature should not be allowed to go below 10°C/50°F.

Water and feeding
It is important never to overwater this plant or let the compost become soggy, so allow it to dry out between waterings. In summer feed with a weak solution at monthly intervals.

Propagation
By seed, which should be planted in a just damp compost with a little extra sand and kept at a constant temperature of 20°C/71°F until established.

Repotting
Repot in spring each year with a good mixture to which a little sand has been added.

PROBLEMS

Relatively problem free, it may suffer from spider mite or scale insect if its location is too warm and dry.

If the leaves droop it has been overwatered. Allow the compost to dry out between waterings.

Brachychiton rupestris can be bought as a bonsai

Caladium bicolor (Angel wings, mother-in-law plant)

QUITE DIFFICULT

This plant is grown for its distinctive heart-shaped variously coloured leaves which are highlighted with contrasting veins and margins. Originally from Central America and Brazil, in its native tropical habitat *Caladium* grows under shady canopy, as its delicate leaves will burn in direct sunlight.

As a houseplant it should be treated as an annual, except by the expert, as it is very fragile and requires high humidity. The plant produces tubers which can be propagated quite easily.

Caladium grows quickly and may produce a green flower at the end of summer. When the leaves die down in autumn, the compost should be kept just moist and warm. In late winter lay the tubers in a new houseplant mixture, place in a bright spot and keep moist and warm. There are marbled and flecked varieties available.

While growing it likes a bright position out of direct sunlight and away from draughts. It needs plenty of humidity, so stand the pot over damp pebbles and mist frequently. Do not wipe the leaves or use leaf shine. Remove any dead or shrivelled leaves by cutting at the stem base.

Handle this plant carefully as it contains a skin irritant.

CARE

Light and temperature
A bright position, but never direct sunlight. During summer the temperature should be 15–18°C/60–64°F, but can go up to 24°C/75°F if the humidity is increased. In winter, keep the temperature around 13°C/55°F and the compost moist while you are overwintering the tubers.

Water and feeding
Water 2–3 times a week in summer, allowing the compost almost to dry out between waterings. Once the plant has stopped growing, reduce the water gradually until winter when the soil should be kept just moist. Ensure humidity by standing the pot over damp pebbles and spraying with tepid water. Feed with a weak solution of liquid fertilizer every 3 weeks while it is growing.

Propagation
In spring by splitting the overwintered tubers. Establish in a propagator in a mixture of soil, peat and sand at a constant temperature of at least 21°C/70°F.

Repotting
Place tubers in a damp mixture of soil, peat and sand in spring. Keep at a temperature of 24°C/75°F until new leaves appear and mist frequently while the plant becomes established.

PROBLEMS

Greenfly is attracted to this plant. Spray with a systemic insecticide.

Take care not to overwater the plant as this will cause mould on the leaves and the top of the compost. Allow to dry out, ensure there are no draughts and water less often.

The plant needs a certain amount of light to maintain leaf colour. If the leaves fade, conditions are too dark.

Shrivelled leaves mean that the compost is too dry or the temperature too hot. Water immediately and keep the plant moist by standing the pot over damp pebbles and spraying frequently.

Caladium bicolor 'Rhoers Dawn'

Chamaedorea elegans (Parlour palm, good luck palm)

EASY

This showy, shade-loving miniature is one of the best palms for growing indoors, its small but sturdy stem producing a cluster of dark green pinnate leathery leaves.

Originally from the mountainous forests of Mexico and Guatemala, where it grows as a ground-cover plant under very tall trees, it has been a popular houseplant for more than one hundred years.

Indoors it will take several years to grow to its mature height of 120cm/4ft.

Chamaedorea elegans produces pale yellow, ball-like flowers that turn into berries throughout the year. These flowers should be cut off as soon as they appear so that they do not weaken the plant.

This plant likes to be kept moist and in a shady position although it will cope with dry atmospheres for shortish periods.

Clean the foliage with a damp cloth and spray occasionally with tepid water.

Chamaedorea elegans lives for up to 10 years indoors and 2 or more plants may be stored in the same pot

CARE

Light and temperature
A semi-shady position, near a window, will suit this plant. It likes temperatures of up to 20°C/68°F in summer and no lower than 13°C/55°F in winter.

Water and feeding
Water 2 or 3 times a week, and in spring and summer feed with a weak solution of liquid fertilizer every 2–3 weeks. If conditions are dry, stand the pot over damp pebbles. In winter allow the compost to dry out between waterings.

Propagation
By seed in spring at a high temperature. Its propagation is difficult and best left to a professional.

Repotting
Repot each spring into a pot one size larger using a loam-based compost.

PROBLEMS

Red spider mite may attack the plant in dry and centrally heated air. Treat with a systemic insecticide.

Take care not to overwater the plant, indicated by the leaves turning brown. Allow the compost almost to dry out before watering again. Trim any leaves which have turned brown.

Equally it should not be underwatered or the leaves will turn yellow. Immerse the pot in water for 30 minutes, drain well and mist frequently.

Chlorophytum comosum 'Variegatum'

(Spider plant, airplane plant, St Bernard's lily)

EASY

This rewarding houseplant is graceful, easy and quick to grow (ideal for a beginner), and should last for many years. It is tolerant of most conditions, even occasional neglect, and can be purchased throughout the year.

Originally from the subtropical areas of South Africa, where it grows in semi-shady, rocky outcrops, it was introduced as a houseplant in the mid-nineteenth century.

Chlorophytum has long, narrow, curving bright green leaves with either a cream centre or cream edges. It produces delicate rosettes of white flowers on long stems and these become independent plants with aerial roots that can be potted on. The parent plant will grow up to 46cm/18in in height and width.

Misting should keep the leaves clean as they are too brittle to wipe. Avoid leaf shine.

Chlorophytum comosum 'Variegatum'

CARE

Light and temperature
A bright or semi-shady, well-ventilated position, away from direct sunlight, with temperatures not above 18°C/64°F in summer or below freezing point in winter. It can tolerate dark places, although leaves are more strongly coloured with bright light.

Water and feeding
Water 2–3 times a week in summer, allowing the soil almost to dry out between waterings, and once a week in winter. Mist daily. Add liquid food to the water every 2 weeks in summer.

Propagation
Roots and stems can be divided, the old soil carefully removed and smaller plants repotted. As the plantlets produce roots, these can be potted on in a small pot beside the parent. When established with new leaves of their own, these plantlets can be cut away from the parent. Alternatively, plantlets can be rooted in water and then potted at any time during the year.

Repotting
Chlorophytum is quite a quick grower and you may need to repot the parent plant twice a year. Use a loam-based mixture, and try not to break the roots when handling the plant.

PROBLEMS

If the plant is looking out of sorts, it may need feeding or is too warm.

Chlorophytum is sensitive to overwatering. If there are brown, slimy marks in the centre of the plant, allow the compost to dry out more between waterings.

The plant also needs plenty of humidity in the form of daily misting or the leaf tips will turn brown or become shrivelled. These tips can be cut off but will go brown again after a few weeks.

Dry air will also attract red spider mite and aphids. Treat spider mite with a systemic insecticide and aphids with pyrethrum based insecticide.

Chrysalidocarpus lutescens

QUITE DIFFICULT (Areca palm, yellow palm, butterfly palm)

This slow-growing member of the palm family has graceful yellow-green pinnate fronds of up to 60cm/2ft long and 1.5cm/½in across which curve from a number of slender yellowish stems.

Originally from Madagascar, and bought commercially from Florida, *Chrysalidocarpus* needs bright but indirect light and warmish, humid conditions. It can withstand cool temperatures, but this will hinder growth. Avoid dry air and mist frequently. It does well in a conservatory.

As a houseplant, in the right conditions, it can grow 20cm/8in a year, reaching 2m/6ft as a mature plant. It should last for many years.

CARE

Light and temperature
Good light, but never direct sunlight. It enjoys a warm temperature of between 18–22°C/ 64–71°F all year round with a maximum of 27°C/80°F in summer and a minimum of 10°C/50°F in winter.

Water and feeding
Water thoroughly, but do not allow the compost to become saturated or to dry out. Feed with a liquid solution every 2 weeks in spring and summer.

Propagation
In spring by seed in a propagator with a constant temperature of 18–20°C/64–68°F. Alternatively, remove basal shoots with some roots and place in a mixture of soil, peat and sand. Cover with plastic and leave in a bright position until established.

Repotting
Repot in spring, only as needed, in the mixture recommended above.

PROBLEMS

Scale insect and red spider mite can attack this plant. Spray with a systemic insecticide and increase humidity by misting frequently.

If the air is too dry the leaves will turn yellow or develop brown spots. Improve moisture and humidity. Remove damaged leaves.

Chrysalidocarpus lutescens produces many suckers at the base of the plant, which can be separated and potted up

Cissus antarctica (Kangaroo vine, kangaroo ivy)

EASY

Cissus antarctica is a quick-growing climber, particularly useful for covering large areas quickly. It also looks good in a hanging basket.

This plant comes from Australia where it grows naturally among the protected undergrowth of the bush in the subtropical areas of New South Wales. As a houseplant it likes a cool position with plenty of water in summer and regular misting to prevent the leaves from turning brown at the edges.

Cissus antarctica has a dense, shrubby base with tendrils that grow to about 3m/9ft in length, which grip easily on to a trellis. It has glossy green oval leaves with brown veins and serrated edges. It is a good idea to pinch out new growth occasionally to encourage a dense plant, though it can easily be pruned back if it does become straggly.

The leaves should be cleaned occasionally with rain water. Do not use leaf shine.

Other popular members of the *Cissus* family are the delicately leaved *C. striata* and the interestingly variegated *C. discolor*.

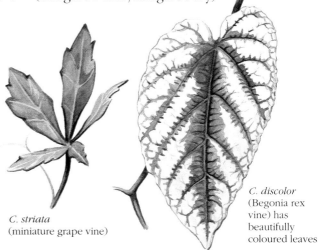

C. striata
(miniature grape vine)

C. discolor
(Begonia rex vine) has beautifully coloured leaves

CARE

Light and temperature
Keep *Cissus antarctica* in strong but indirect light. The ideal summer temperature is 18–21°C/64–70°F, and in winter no lower than 12°C/54°F.

Water and feeding
Water 2–3 times a week in summer, allowing the compost almost to dry out between waterings. In winter keep the compost just moist and water only every 2 weeks. Add a little liquid fertilizer at fortnightly intervals in summer.

Propagation
In spring using stem-tip cuttings with new growth which will root easily in a mixture of compost and sand. Cover the pot with plastic and put in a warm spot with suffused light until the new plants become established.

Repotting
If the plant is growing vigorously you may need to repot it twice a year. Once it reaches the desired height you can keep it in the same pot and just change the topsoil in spring.

PROBLEMS

If webs appear on the underside of the leaves the plant has been attacked by red spider mite. Spray with systemic insecticide and improve humidity.

Greenfly will cause the leaves to become distorted. Spray with a pyrethrum-based insecticide.

Brown or brittle leaves mean that the plant is too dry and hot. Water and mist well and move to a cooler position.

Take care not to overwater the plant or the leaves will develop brown spots and become mildewy. Check that the drainage is adequate and allow the compost to dry out between waterings. Mildew can be treated with a benomyl-based fungicide.

Cissus antarctica 'Ellen Danica'

Cocos nucifera (Coconut palm)

QUITE DIFFICULT

This exotic, slow-growing plant is a familiar sight along the beaches of South East Asia, the Pacific and Central and Southern America. Its trunk – up to 30m/90ft in height – is topped with feathery fronds which lean out towards the sea. At its base lie large edible nuts contained in brown husks.

Cocos nucifera has been specially cultivated as a houseplant. In the pot the plant is attached to the coconut seed, its glossy palm-like leaves growing from a short stem.

Indoors it can reach up to 3m/9ft, but the first 2–3 years are the most difficult in the plant's life. It does much better in a conservatory than it does in the average room, but once over the first 3 years it can live for a long time.

However the chances of getting any nuts in captivity, so to speak, are remote.

Ensure that the plant has adequate humidity – it does not like dry air – and try to give it a spell outdoors in a protected spot in summer.

Cocos nucifera

CARE

Light and temperature
A bright, warm position, with occasional direct sunlight. The ideal temperature is 18–21°C/64–70°F all year round, and no lower than 15°C/60°F in winter.

Water and feeding
The plant needs regular watering, but allow the compost to dry out between waterings. To ensure adequate humidity, stand the pot over damp pebbles and mist daily with tepid water. Feed with a liquid fertilizer at monthly intervals in spring and summer.

Propagation
This is difficult and best left to a professional.

Repotting
This will be necessary only if the plant outgrows its pot. Use a small container and make sure the nut remains above the surface of the soil. Use a mixture of 3 parts soil, 2 parts peat and 1 part sand.

PROBLEMS

Relatively problem free unless its conditions are too dry, which will cause the leaf tips to turn brown. Water and mist well, and stand the pot over damp gravel. You may have to move it to a better position.

White woolly patches on the leaves and white grubs in the soil indicate mealy bug. Spray malathion on to the leaves and water it into the soil according to the manufacturer's recommendations.

Webs on the underside of the leaves indicate red spider mite. Spray with a systemic insecticide and check watering and humidity is adequate.

Codiaeum (Joseph's coat)

QUITE DIFFICULT

Originally from the tropical areas of Malaysia and Indonesia, this most colourful but fragile houseplant has been popular since it was introduced in the mid-nineteenth century.

Its smooth, laurel-shaped, variegated leaves range in colour from green to yellow, orange and red, with mottled or striped yellow markings. It can grow into quite a large shrub, around 1m/3ft tall and across. *Codiaeum* requires constant humid conditions, away from draughts and central heating. Strong light is needed to maintain colour in the leaves; however the plant should not be sprayed while it is in sunlight or the leaves will burn.

The plant rests in winter and loses many of its bottom leaves, so it is often treated as an annual, though the experienced grower can expect it to live for many years and can ensure a bushy plant by removing the growing tips.

Codiaeum 'Gold King'

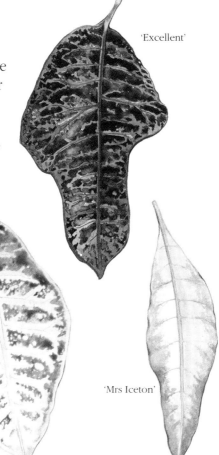

'Excellent'

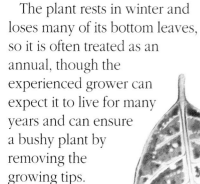

'Norma'

'Mrs Iceton'

CARE

Light and temperature
Bright, and occasionally direct, sunlight and a constant temperature all year no lower than 16°C/61°F.

Water and feeding
In summer water 2–3 times a week. Take care never to let the plant dry out. In winter use tepid water every 4–5 days. Spray occasionally to provide humidity and keep the leaves clean. Stand the pot over damp gravel. Feed with a liquid fertilizer every 2 weeks in summer.

Propagation
In spring by stem-tip cuttings using a propagator at a temperature of about 24°C/75°F. The plant yields a milky juice so sprinkle the cuttings in charcoal powder to seal the 'wound' before planting. Use gloves while handling the plant as the juice contains an irritant.

Repotting
In late spring, annually or as needed, in a loam-based compost. Pack tightly, but ensure good drainage.

PROBLEMS

Prone to red spider mite. Spray with a systemic insecticide and improve humidity. Also scale insect and mealy bug. Remove these with a cloth dipped in methylated spirit.

If the bottom leaves drop off, the conditions are too dry or cold or fluctuating. Move to a warmer spot where the conditions are more easily controllable.

Brown tips and shrivelled leaves are caused by hot, dry air or underwatering. Immerse the pot in water for 10 minutes, drain well, and do not allow the compost to dry out. Improve humidity by standing the pot over damp gravel and spraying frequently. The plant may also need to be moved to a cooler position. Damaged leaves can be cut off.

Overwatering will cause stem rot, recognizable by brown patches on the stem and a drooping of the leaves. Allow the compost to dry out and water less.

Coffea arabica (Arabian coffee plant, coffee tree of commerce)

EASY

Coffea arabica is closely related to Gardenia

The coffee plant adapts well to indoors and can be expected to grow to 1–2m/3–6ft in height. It has a single stem which in time becomes thick and bushy, especially if the growing tips are removed regularly.

The glossy, oval-shaped, pointed leaves are an attractive dark green and are prominently veined. Mature indoor plants will produce star-shaped white flowers in late summer which turn into green and eventually red berries containing coffee beans.

This plant is originally from the subtropical areas of Ethiopia, where it grows at a high altitude in quite cool temperatures. Indoors it needs a very moist atmosphere, so mist the plant frequently and place the pot over wet gravel. It must never be allowed to dry out completely.

Coffea arabica rests briefly in winter and may lose its leaves. At this time keep it barely damp and well away from central heating and draughts. Prune to keep the plant shapely.

The plant should last for 5–6 years.

CARE

Light and temperature
Bright but indirect light, away from direct sunlight. In summer the ideal temperature is 18–22°C/64–71°F. In winter a minimum of 8°C/45°F will be tolerated if the plant is kept quite dry.

Water and feeding
Water 2–3 times a week in spring and summer, but do not allow the plant to stand in water or to become soggy. Spray frequently. In winter water much less, especially if the surrounding temperature is cold, allowing the compost almost to dry out between waterings. Feed fortnightly with a liquid solution in spring and summer.

Propagation
Specially purchased seeds can be sown in spring and kept at 24°C/75°F in a propagator, in a mixture of loam, peat and sand. Place in a greenhouse or under a plastic cover in diffused light until established.

Repotting
Each spring in a mixture of loam, peat and sand, ensuring good drainage.

PROBLEMS

Relatively problem free, but prone to scale insect and mealy bug, especially if conditions are too dry. Spray with a systemic insecticide and improve humidity.

The leaves will wilt and may go yellow if the plant is overwatered or allowed to become soggy. Let it dry out and then water a little less.

Coleus blumei (Flame nettle)

EASY

This cultivated hybrid is grown for its highly coloured leaves. If the growing tips are pinched out regularly it should become an attractive, bushy plant of 60cm/2ft. It was introduced from Java in 1853.

Indoors it is often grown as an annual because it is quick-growing and easy to propagate. If the plant becomes very tired in winter and you wish to keep it rather than propagate, it can be cut back in spring to within 7.5cm/3in of the compost. *Coleus blumei* likes a moist atmosphere and needs direct light to keep its colours strong and its foliage in good condition.

Coleus blumei

Four of the numerous *Coleus blumei* hybrids

CARE

Light and temperature
Bright, direct sunlight with a warm temperature, ideally around 21°C/70°F. It will withstand temperatures of around 10°C/50°F, but likes slightly higher, preferably not below 13°C/55°F.

Water and feeding
Coleus needs moist, humid conditions so the soil should always be kept damp and the pot stood over wet gravel. Mist often. Keep the compost drier in winter. Feed with a liquid solution every 2 weeks, except in winter.

Propagation
Cut the plant back during winter and keep the compost quite dry. In early spring encourage new growth by watering and fertilizing. Take tip cuttings and place in a damp no. 1 compost. Keep in a shady spot at a temperature of 18°C/64°F.

Repotting
Repot in summertime as the plant outgrows its pot. To check this, remove the plant from the pot and see if it is rootbound.

PROBLEMS

If the temperature is too cool or there is insufficient water or moisture the plant will lose its leaves.

Prone to red spider mite in dry conditions. Remove individually with a cloth soaked in methylated spirit and improve humidity.

Crassula argentea (Jade tree, money plant)

EASY

Originally from South Africa, this attractive succulent has glossy, dark green, fleshy leaves which grow from a tree-like trunk. It may produce pretty pink or white flowers in spring, which are shortlived.

Crassula makes an ideal houseplant as it likes the warm, dry atmosphere of a centrally heated home and does not require much attention. It should live for a good number of years.

In summer it should be watered regularly, but drained well. Mist occasionally to clean the leaves. In winter it much prefers a cool, dry place to rest.

Crassula is a slow grower, but can be everlasting so it is worthwhile investing in an attractive and sturdy pot. The adult plant should reach 1m/3ft in height. If it is necessary to prune the plant, dust the 'wound' with sulphur to stem the flow of its sap.

It enjoys a spell outside in summer in a sunny but protected position.

CARE

Light and temperature
Crassula needs sunlight. In summer it can withstand almost any amount of heat. In winter the temperature should be cool, but not below 5–7°C/40–45°F. Keep the compost almost dry at this time.

Water and feeding
In summer water 2–3 times a week; in winter once a month should suffice. Feed every 2 weeks in summer with a high-potash fertilizer into the compost or sprayed on the leaves.

Propagation
Usually by seed in a propagator or by stem cuttings, with a growing point and some leaves, which will root easily in a good seeding mixture at room temperature after they have been allowed to dry out for a few days.

Repotting
Only when necessary, probably every 2 years, using a loam-based compost mixed with sand.

PROBLEMS

If the plant does not grow it may need feeding. Also check to see if it is rootbound and needs repotting.

Growth may also be hindered if there are any white woolly patches on the roots, caused by mealy bug. If so, drench the roots with diluted malathion.

If the stems become elongated, the plant is being kept in too shady a place.

If the plant turns black and rotten at the base it has been overwatered and will probably die. Try cutting out the rot and dusting with sulphur.

Crassula will lose its leaves and condition if left in too warm a spot in winter. Move to a cooler, dry place.

Crassula argentea is a succulent cultivated as an indoor plant since the 1830s

Cryptanthus (Starfish plant, earth star)

EASY

Cryptanthus is an ideal houseplant as it thrives in the sun and if treated well is almost problem free.

Originally from Brazil, it grows as an epiphyte in dry thorn forests. It is actually a member of the bromeliad family (see page 119), though atypically it does not store its own water. Its root system is shallow and it can easily be wired on to bark or a log to imitate its native habitat, but care must be taken to ensure it does not dry out.

The plant forms a star-shaped rosette of spiny, arched, pink or brown leaves with wavy cream stripes running across. Small cream flowers may bloom throughout the year. These are concealed within the foliage and account for the plant's genus name, which in Greek means 'hidden flower'.

It is a slow grower, but should last indefinitely.

Top: *Cryptanthus forsterianus*; middle: *Cryptanthus tricolor*; bottom: *Cryptanthus bivattatus*

C. fosterianus (stiff pheasant leaf) is the largest variety

C. bromeliades 'Tricolor' (rainbow star)

CARE

Light and temperature
Bright, sunny conditions throughout the year with warm temperatures of between 20–22°C/68–72°F.

Water and feeding
Provide humidity by standing the pot on damp gravel and misting frequently with rain water. Water the soil sufficiently to keep it moist and allow it to dry out between waterings. Feed every 3–4 weeks in summer with a weak solution.

Propagation
In spring by detaching any well-formed lateral shoots and potting them in a damp mixture of orchid compost. Cover with clear plastic and place in bright but indirect light for about 3 months, then repot in a small container filled with a pure peat mix.

Repotting
Seldom, except for propagation, as the pot only provides support for the plant. They have largish root systems.

PROBLEMS

Leaves will shrivel or turn brown if the atmosphere is too hot or dry. Spray and water regularly as this plant needs a lot of humidity. Trim off the damaged sections of the leaves.

The plant will rot at the base if it is too cold and wet. Allow it to dry out and water less.

Dull leaves indicate lack of light. Spray and move to a warmer position.

Ctenanthe oppenheimiana

QUITE DIFFICULT (Never-never plant)

This Brazilian plant is much sought after for the unusual dark green markings on its pale green foliage. An attractive plant, it has long stalks that produce large pointed elliptical leaves of up to 30cm/12in long which are red underneath.

Its native habitat is the Alto de Sena region in South East Brazil, which has 350–400cm/140–160in of rain per year. It grows along the escarpments of this wet coastal range and is found underneath the low tree canopy of these dripping forests.

Ctenanthe is a good houseplant because it enjoys average room temperatures and has no particular needs. As long as it is not overwatered and has adequate humidity in the form of misting and standing the pot over damp gravel, it should do well. Indoors it should grow to 1m/3ft high and wide.

The plant has a dormant period in winter when it will simply need to be kept warm and the compost prevented from drying out.

It should last for 5–6 years, becoming an attractively bushy plant.

CARE

Light and temperature
Semi-shade during summer at 18–21°C/64–70°F, but it will accept temperatures up to 29°C/85°F. In winter it prefers more light and will withstand temperatures as low as 10°C/50°F if kept almost dry.

Water and feeding
Water thoroughly in spring and summer. Place the pot over pebbles almost covered with water as this plant enjoys high humidity coupled with warm temperatures. Spray daily. Feed every 2 weeks with general houseplant fertilizer from early spring to end of summer. During winter water once a week and less if the temperature drops to 10°C/50°F.

Propagation
In spring from stem cuttings with several leaves. Treat with a rooting powder and pot in a mixture of peat and sand. Cover with plastic or place in a greenhouse at 21°C/70°F until established.

Repotting
In spring in a no. 2 peat-based compost.

PROBLEMS

Mealy bug, scale insect and red spider mite can attack this plant. Spray mealy bug with diluted malathion and scale insect and spider mite with a systemic insecticide.

Hot, dry conditions will cause the leaves to curl. Water well and increase humidity by misting and standing the pot over damp gravel.

If the position is too cold in winter the plant will suffer root rot. Allow to dry out, water less frequently and move to a warmer position.

Ctenanthe lubbersiana has a more upright habit than *C.O. tricolor*

Cupressus (Monterey cypress)

QUITE EASY

This Southern Californian conifer has recently become a popular houseplant. It is quick-growing and can be pruned easily to enhance its natural pyramid shape.

Cupressus can be seen growing along the coastal areas of California, its spreading branches supporting a canopy of bright to dark green needles.

It is easy to grow indoors as long as it has plenty of indirect light and its compost is never allowed to dry out or become soggy. It should be misted occasionally.

The plant should last for many years.

CARE

Light and temperature
Bright but not direct sunlight. The ideal temperature in summer is 18–22°C/64–72°F, with a cooler temperature of 5–10°C/41–50°F in winter.

Water and feeding
Keep moist but never soggy at all times. In winter it will need less water, but must never be allowed to dry out. Feed with a liquid solution every 4 weeks in spring and summer. Mist occasionally.

Propagation
By stem cuttings in spring. Propagating this plant is quite difficult and best left to professionals.

Repotting
As needed, probably every second year, in a mixture of no. 2 soil-based compost.

PROBLEMS

If conditions are too warm and dry, red spider mite will attack the plant. Remove with a cloth soaked in methylated spirit.

Cupressus macrocarpa is rewarding because of its vigorous growth

Cycas revoluta (Sago palm)

EASY

This exotic palm is extremely slow-growing and therefore usually quite expensive.

Originally from South East Asia and Japan, where it grows under canopy, it has a stout pineapple-shaped stem from which project feathery evergreen fronds of up to 1m/3ft in length. The plant will usually produce one of these a year. Its mature height is around 2m/6ft, and it will last 50 or 60 years.

Cycas likes bright, indirect sunlight, thrives in normal room temperatures and does not need much humidity.

Mature plants benefit from a spell outdoors in summer if conditions are warm. Even so it will not flower.

CARE

Light and temperature
Strong but indirect light. It likes average room temperatures – 18–22°C/64–72°F – throughout the year, though it is fairly resistant to occasional cool temperatures and can tolerate as low as 5–10°C/41–50°F.

Water and feeding
Water moderately all year, enough to keep the compost moist but never let it dry out or become soggy. Feed once a month in spring and summer with a weak solution.

Propagation
In spring by seed or by potting basal roots in a seed compost. Establish in a propagator at 30°C/86°F. This process is quite difficult and best left to professionals.

Repotting
Repot every 2–3 years in spring or autumn in a mixture of soil, peat and sand.

PROBLEMS

Red spider mite and scale insect tend to attack this plant. Spray with a systemic insecticide and move to a cooler position.

Cycas revoluta is one of the most primitive flowering plants

Cyperus papyrus (Egyptian paper plant)

DIFFICULT

In ancient Egypt this exotic plant was used for making papyrus.

As a houseplant it grows to 2–3m/6–10ft, with large clusters of long, smooth stems topped with dense thread-like bracts which can produce a large umbrellate flower.

Originally from the marshy river banks of the Mediterranean, it is a demanding houseplant as it needs bright conditions, a lot of moisture and warm winter temperatures. In fact, it is impossible to give this plant too much moisture.

It is long lasting if the conditions are right.

CARE

Light and temperature
Bright light and high temperatures of up to 20–24°C/68–75°F. In winter the temperature should be no lower than 13°C/55°F.

Water and feeding
Cyperus must always be kept very moist and the pot should be stood in a shallow bowl of water so that the compost and roots are always damp. Spray frequently. Use a liquid fertilizer every 2 weeks.

Propagation
Easily by division of clumps. Remove the plant from the pot and break the rootball into sections. Cut off the tips of the leaves on one stem and bend the stem so the leaves are submerged in water. New plants emanate from the old leaf. Change the water every 5 days.

Repotting
In spring, in a mixture if soil, peat and sand, in a smallish pot.

PROBLEMS

The tips of the bracts will turn brown if the plant is too dry. Stand the pot in water. Trim the damaged needles.

Insufficient light will stop growth. Move to a better position.

Prone to whitefly and greenfly. Spray with a pyrethrum-based insecticide.

Cyperus alternifolius 'Zimula'

61

Dieffenbachia (Dumb cane, leopard lily)

Dieffenbachia picta 'Marianne' is one of the spotted dumb canes

QUITE DIFFICULT

This ornamental houseplant originally came from the tropical rain forests of Colombia, Costa Rica and Venezuela. Growing from a thick stem are elongated dark green leaves which are attractively variegated with creamy yellow in the centre.

As a houseplant it grows up to 1m/3ft. It is a quick grower and can last for a long time, though as the plant becomes older it sheds its lower leaves and is best replaced after 3–4 years.

It requires constant and warm conditions, like those it enjoys in its native habitat, and will do well in central heating as long as it is misted daily and the pot stood over damp gravel. It also benefits from a spell outdoors in summer in a shady spot. It does not like draughts, so make sure it is placed in a protected position.

Dieffenbachia produces a poisonous sap, so always wear gloves when handling the plant.

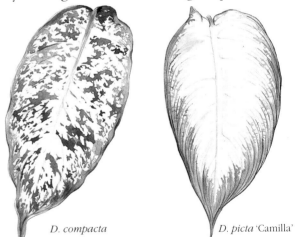

D. compacta   *D. picta* 'Camilla'

CARE

Light and temperature
This plant thrives in a shady position with a little indirect light. The ideal temperature is around 18°C/64°F. If above 20°C/70°F it will need even more humidity. Do not let the temperature go below 10°C/50°F.

Water and feeding
Water well in summer, probably every second day, as the compost must always be kept moist, but never soggy. In winter water less as the plant will not be growing and soil should be allowed almost to dry out between waterings. Feed every 2 weeks in summer with a liquid fertilizer.

Propagation
By stem-tip cuttings just below a node. Treat the base with a rooting powder and bury the cuttings in a pot filled with damp peat and sand. Place in a greenhouse or wrap in plastic and keep in bright light at a constant temperature of 21–24°C/70–75°F until established. It can also be propagated by cutting the stem into 7–8cm/3in sections and burying in the same medium.

Repotting
In spring, in a mixture of organic soil, peat and sand.

PROBLEMS

Prone to stem rot, indicated by a slimy stem. Do not allow the plant to get too wet. Dust damaged areas with sulphur and take care not to overwater.

Overwatering will also cause the leaves to turn yellow. Allow the compost to dry out and water less.

If the lower leaves droop, the position is too cold. Move to a warmer spot.

Dionaea muscipula (Venus fly trap)

VERY DIFFICULT

A fascinating insectivorous perennial with clusters of dainty rosettes that have spiny leaves hinged in the middle, which close over and kill any insect attracted by its juices. The action is immediate. It has adapted thus, being unable to get nutrition from other sources.

It is a small plant, growing to a maximum height of 7.5–20cm/3–8in. White flowers will appear in summer.

Dionaea muscipula comes from the temperate areas of the Carolinas in North America where it grows in mossy and marshy surroundings. As a houseplant it will require similar conditions to its native habitat – a bright but cool, damp spot with a lot of humidity.

It is a difficult plant to grow indoors and has a dormant period in winter.

Dionaea muscipula

CARE

Light and temperature
Bright but indirect light and a cool, damp position, with temperatures no lower than 10°C/50°F in winter.

Water and feeding
It likes damp conditions and fresh rain water, so the pot should be stood in a shallow container of rain water, and the compost kept moist at all times; never let it dry out. In winter cover the pot with plastic and keep the compost just moist.

Feed occasionally with very small bits of meat or dead insects.

Propagation
In autumn plant seeds in a damp, peaty compost mixed with moss. Cover with plastic until established. Alternatively the rhizome can be divided in spring and each piece placed into its own pot, then covered with plastic until established.

Repotting
Not necessary.

PROBLEMS

Although relatively pest-free, it is difficult to grow as conditions must be as close as possible to its natural habitat in order for the plant to thrive.

It must never be allowed to dry out otherwise the plant will die. Stand in a pot filled with a little water at all times.

In winter, when there are no flies, feed with small pieces of meat.

Dizygotheca elegantissima (False aralia, finger aralia)

QUITE DIFFICULT

A pretty shrub from the tropical islands of the New Hebrides, *Dizygotheca elegantissima* has a slim mottled stem from which grow palm-like, leathery, serrated leaves of around 7.5cm/3in long and 1cm/½in wide. These leaves are reddish-brown when young and dark green when mature.

In its native habitat it grows on the steamy mountainside along with crotons, cycas, cordylines and epipremnums. Indoors it needs similiar conditions, so to ensure plenty of humidity stand the pot over damp pebbles and mist frequently. It will do best in a greenhouse or conservatory.

The plant can be pruned to improve its shape and bushiness.

A mature specimen will grow to 1.5m/4–5ft tall and should last for up to 5 years.

CARE

Light and temperature
Bright but indirect light. The temperature should always be warm, with a summer maximum of 24°C/75°F and a winter minimum of 15°C/60°F when the plant is dormant.

Water and feeding
Immerse the pot in water for 30 minutes and drain well, allowing the compost almost to dry out between waterings. Feed at fortnightly intervals in spring and summer with a liquid solution. In winter water less, but do not allow the plant to dry out completely.

Propagation
Difficult. It is best left to a professional.

Repotting
In spring, as needed, into a pot the next size up. Use a no. 2 peat-based compost.

PROBLEMS

If the plant is overwatered, the foliage will droop, and if it is underwatered, it will lose its leaves. Follow the instructions in 'Water and feeding' carefully.

If the conditions are too dry, the plant will start to look unhealthy. Water well and improve the humidity by standing the pot over damp pebbles and misting daily.

Greenfly tends to attack this plant. Treat with a pyrethrum-based insecticide.

White woolly patches on the leaves and stems indicate mealy bug. Remove with a cloth dipped in methylated spirit.

Dizygotheca elegantissima, sometimes sold as *D. laciniata*, should be planted 2 or 3 to a pot for maximum effect

Dracaena deremensis (Striped dracaena)

QUITE EASY

Originally from the tropical areas of Africa, where its native habitat is under the tree canopy, this elegant shrubby plant has sword-shaped, grey-green striped leaves, with white margins running along the edge, that grow up to 45cm/18in long and 5cm/2in wide.

It likes a protected spot with reasonable light, good humidity and warm temperatures.

Often mistaken for a member of the palm family, *Dracaena deremensis* can grow to 4m/12ft in a relatively dark location. It is a slow grower, but should live for 7–8 years, though the bottom leaves will tend to wither, showing the cane stem.

Dracaena deremensis 'Janet Craig'

D. d. 'Lemon Lime'   *D. d.* 'White Stripe'

CARE

Light and temperature
A reasonable amount of light is needed to maintain the colour in the leaves, though it can do well in a shady position. It likes fairly high temperatures, of around 18–24°C/64–75°F, no lower than 12°C/53°F in winter when it has a resting period.

Water and feeding
Water 2–3 times a week while the plant is growing, but do not let the compost get soggy and do not stand the pot in water. When dormant, water sparingly and allow the compost almost to dry out between waterings. Feed at fortnightly intervals in spring and summer with a liquid solution.

Propagation
From basal shoots, tip or stem cuttings. Plant in a mixture of peat and sand, cover with plastic and keep at a constant temperature of around 20–24°C/71–75°F until established.

PROBLEMS

If the lower leaves droop, the plant is too hot and dry. Water well and spray frequently.

If there is no new growth, the plant needs feeding.

Spots on the leaves are caused by a fungal parasite. Treat with a systemic fungicide.

Scale insect and mealy bug are attracted to this plant. Remove with a cloth dipped in methylated spirit.

If the leaves become faded with webbing on the underside, red spider mite has attacked the plant. Spray with a systemic insecticide and improve humidity.

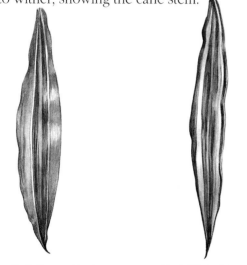

Dracaena deremensis 'Warneckii' has 2 stripes

Dracaena fragrans 'Massangeana' (Dragon tree)

EASY

A popular and hardy house-plant, *Dracaena fragrans* 'Massangeana' will withstand a variety of temperatures and conditions as long as it has adequate humidity. The wide yellow stripe is bordered by narrower yellow lines.

It comes originally from the eastern part of Africa, Sierra Leone and Ethiopia, where it is to be found growing in brick-red soil on the moist slopes and humid valleys of the mountains, especially the Ucambaras. As a houseplant it will reach 1.5m/ 4–5ft in height if given the right conditions.

The plant has rosettes of strong green curving leaves with a central yellow stripe. As it grows it loses its lower leaves, to show a stout bare stem.

Indoors *Dracaena fragrans* likes bright, filtered light, average room temperatures and plenty of humidity, so the pot should be placed over damp pebbles and the plant misted frequently, though not while it is in sunlight.

It does not like draughts so stand in a protected spot.

The plant is a relatively slow grower and should last for several years.

Dracaena fragrans 'Massangeana'

CARE

Light and temperature
It needs plenty of light to bring out the colour in its leaves, but keep the plant out of the midday sun. Ideally it likes warm temperatures of between 18–21°C/ 64–71°F, though it is fairly flexible and will tolerate as low as 13°C/55°F with less frequent watering.

Water and feeding
Water once or twice a week in summer and once a week in winter. Avoid sogginess, but never allow the compost to dry out completely. Feed with a liquid solution every 2 weeks in summer.

Propagation
In spring by stem-tip cuttings or stem sections cut to 8cm/3in long. Establish in a humid propagator at 24°C/75°F.

Repotting
In spring every 2–3 years in a loam- or peat-based compost, ensuring good drainage.

PROBLEMS

It is natural for the plant to lose its lower leaves gradually, but if they are showing signs of drooping generally, the conditions are too dry and hot. Water well and spray.

Brownish spots on the leaves denote botrytis, meaning the plant is possibly too cold and damp. Spray with fungicide, move to a warmer place and allow the surface of the soil to dry out between waterings. You should also remove the damaged leaves.

If the plant is overwatered the leaves and stem will rot. Allow to dry out and water less.

Prone to scale insect and red spider mite. Spray with a systemic insecticide and improve humidity.

Dracaena marginata (Madagascar dragon tree)

QUITE EASY

This exotic-looking plant is the easiest *Dracaena* to grow indoors as it is tolerant of varying room conditions and different degrees of humidity.

The young plant produces leaves from the base. Gradually over the years the lower leaves fall so, as the plant grows, it develops several slender, ringed trunks which produce dense tufts of spiky green leaves with reddish edgings. *D. m.* 'Tricolor', a more recent introduction, has pink, cream and green striped leaves.

In its native habitat, Madagascar, it is quite a substantial specimen, growing to a height of 3m/9ft. Indoors it will reach 2m/6ft, gradually losing its basal leaves, giving the plant its distinctively marked stem.

It should last for several years. In warmer climates it likes a spell outdoors in summer in a sheltered position.

D. m. tricolor was introduced in the 1970s and is a splendidly coloured plant

CARE

Light and temperature
The plant needs a reasonable amount of light to keep the colour in its leaves and requires temperatures of 18–21°C/64–71°F all year, though it will withstand temperatures as low as 13°C/55°F in winter.

Water and feeding
Water 2–3 times a week in summer and spray frequently. In winter, when the plant is dormant, water less and allow the soil almost to dry out between waterings. Feed at fortnightly intervals with a liquid solution in spring and summer.

Propagation
By stem-tip cuttings or stem sections cut to 8cm/3in lengths. Place in a no. 2 peat-based compost and establish in a propagator at 24°C/75°F.

Repotting
For the first 2 years repot each spring in a no. 2 peat-based compost. Thereafter every other year, finishing up in a 20–25cm/8–10in pot, replacing the top 7.5cm/3in of compost annually.

PROBLEMS

If conditions are too dry, the lower leaves will droop. Water and spray more often.

If the position is too cold the plant will lose its leaves and stop growing. Move to a better location.

If there is no new growth in spring the plant needs feeding.

White woolly patches on the leaves and stems indicate mealy bug. Remove with a cloth dipped in methylated spirit or spray with diluted malathion.

Dracaena marginata

D. m. colorama is a more recent introduction and equally adaptable and easy to grow

Dracaena reflexa (Song of India)

QUITE DIFFICULT

This ornamental *Dracaena* comes from the monsoon forests and mangrove swamps of India and Sri Lanka, where it is found under the tree canopy growing to 4m/12ft if given support.

It has beautiful, broad, creamy-yellow arched leaves, with a central green stripe, that grow up to 15cm/6in long.

It is a sensitive houseplant and a slow grower. A mature specimen will reach 1m/3ft in height with a spread of 50cm/18in. It should last for many years, though it will shed its lower leaves.

Although it likes plenty of humidity, take care not to overwater the plant and do not repot it too often. Stand the pot over a saucer of damp pebbles.

Dracaena reflexa

CARE

Light and temperature
Bright but indirect light and warm temperatures, not below 18°C/64°F, all year.

Water and feeding
Keep just moist, avoiding sogginess and never letting the compost dry out. Feed every 2 weeks in spring and summer with a liquid solution.

Propagation
By top cuttings. Establish in a propagator at a constant temperature of 25°C/77°F.

Repotting
Do not repot this plant very often, every 3 years is recommended.

PROBLEMS

The plant will shed its lower leaves naturally as it grows.

Take care to ensure good humidity as dry conditions, especially central heating, will cause browned edges on the leaves. Water carefully and mist frequently.

Watch for mealy bugs and treat with a swab dipped in methylated spirit.

Epipremnum aureum (Devil's ivy)

EASY

This plant is also commonly known as *Scindapsus aureus*. A vigorous climber, it comes from the humid tropical Solomon and South East Asian islands, where it attaches itself to the bark of host tree trunks.

It is easy to grow indoors and as a houseplant its aerial roots can be trained to cover a moss pole to a height of 1–1.5m/3–5ft, or its tendrils can look good trailing over a hanging basket. The plant can also be grown in water.

Epipremnum has glossy green leaves covered with yellow patches or spots. These will gradually fade and should be removed from the stem. Pinch out new shoots occasionally to ensure dense growth. It needs warm, humid conditions and should be sprayed frequently with tepid water.

Wash your hands after handling the plant as the leaves contain an irritant.

Epipremnum aureum
'Marble Queen'

Epipremnum aureum

CARE

Light and temperature
Bright indirect light with temperatures around 18–24°C/64–75°F all year, and never below 13°C/55°F.

Water and feeding
In spring and summer water 2–3 times a week, allowing the soil to dry out between waterings. Good drainage is essential for this plant. Water less in winter. Spray frequently. Use a liquid fertilizer every 2 weeks in spring and summer.

Propagation
In spring from stem-tip cuttings 10cm/4in long. Allow to root in water and then plant in the mixture recommended below.

Repotting
Every other year in a peat-based no. 2 compost.

PROBLEMS

Ensure good drainage and avoid overwatering as the plant can develop stem rot. Allow the compost to dry out and water less frequently.

If the position is too damp or dark there may be root rot and leaf drop. Move to a brighter position.

White woolly patches on the leaves indicate mealy bug. Remove with a cloth dipped in methylated spirit or spray with diluted malathion.

Euonymus japonica (Japanese spindle tree)

QUITE DIFFICULT

Originally from Japan, where it is found by the sea and is often used for hedges, *Euonymus japonica* is a multiple-branched evergreen with either fine leathery leaves with white edges or dark green glossy leaves 3–5cm/1–2in long which have central yellow patches. In late spring it may develop small white flowers.

As a houseplant it will grow up to 1m/3ft. It can be made into quite a bushy specimen if the growing shoots are regularly pinched out.

It is a hardy houseplant. It likes good light, but tolerates very cold rooms. If kept in a heated room it will probably shed its leaves in winter.

Place the plant outdoors for a spell in early summer. After it has passed its best indoors it can be moved into the garden in summer where it will make an attractive shrub.

Euonymus japonica 'Argenteo', the silver queen

CARE

Light and temperature
Bright but indirect light and cool temperatures suit this plant. In winter it benefits from 3–4 hours of sunshine daily. The ideal temperature is between 13–16°C/55–61°F, a little higher if it is stood over a bowl of wet pebbles.

Water and feeding
Water well in summer, letting the topsoil dry out between waterings. In winter water sparingly, but ensure it doesn't dry out completely. Mist leaves occasionally. Feed with liquid fertilizer at fortnightly intervals in spring and summer.

Propagation
In spring take tip cuttings 7.5cm/3in long, dust with rooting hormone, place in a mixture of soil, peat and sand, and keep at between 21–24°C/70–75°F in filtered light until established.

Repotting
In spring using a mixture of soil, peat and sand, but only when the plant has outgrown its container.

PROBLEMS

Cobwebs underneath the leaves indicate red spider mite. It can also be attacked by aphids and scale insect. Spray with a systemic insecticide.

Leaf drop may occur if the plant is kept in too warm a spot during winter.

Mildew is a common problems with this plant. If it appears on the leaves, spray with a fungicide.

Euphorbia trigona (Spurge)

EASY

This cactus-like succulent grows upright stout stems which produce lateral rows of thorny leaves.

Originally from the arid areas of Africa, it is a most undemanding houseplant, requiring only good light and a little water in order to thrive indoors. It does, however, benefit from a spell outside in summer on a warm patio.

The plant produces a poisonous juice so it should be handled with care and kept out of the reach of children and animals.

CARE

Light and temperature
Bright, even direct, sunlight with temperatures between 15–18°C/60–64°F all year.

Water and feeding
This plant does not need a lot of water. In spring and summer water only once a week and in winter only occasionally by submerging the pot in water for 15 minutes and then allowing it to drain. The top of the compost should dry out between waterings. In spring and summer feed monthly with a weak solution.

Propagation
By cuttings. Run tepid water over the cutting until the sap has stopped flowing. Allow to dry and plant in a compost for cactus.

Repotting
Only as necessary in a cactus potting mixture.

PROBLEMS

This plant is relatively problem free.

Always use gloves when handling.

Euphorbia trigona 'Hermentiona'

Fatshedera lizei (Ivy tree)

'Variegata'

EASY

This hybrid, a cross between *Fatsia japonica* and *Hedera helix*, was created in France in 1910 and retains the best features of both species. It is a climber, up to a height of 1–1.5m/3–5ft, and usually needs support in the form of a stake or moss pole.

It has glossy dark green leaves with five lobes, and mature plants may produce small green flowers.

Fatshedera is quite a hardy plant, but it must not be overwatered or allowed to dry out. Spray regularly and if it is in a centrally heated room stand the pot over damp pebbles. Indoors it will tolerate quite dark conditions, though it prefers good light, which will improve the appearance of the plant. Pinch out the new growth to encourage bushiness and wash the leaves occasionally with a damp cloth. Do not use leaf shine.

It should last for several years, at which point you may wish to propagate a new plant.

'Anna Michels'

Fatshedera lizei 'Pia'

CARE

Light and temperature
A well-lit room and quite cool temperatures – as low as 7°C/45°F in winter and not above 18°C/64°F in summer.

Water and feeding
Water 2–3 times a week in summer, but do not allow the pot to stand in water or the compost to become soggy. Water less in winter, especially if the temperature is low, but take care not to let it dry out. Use a houseplant fertilizer every 2 weeks in spring and summer.

Propagation
In spring root stem-tip cuttings of 10–15cm/4–6in in water. Cover with plastic and establish at a minimum temperature of 13°C/55°F in filtered light.

Repotting
A young plant should be repotted in spring in a no. 2 peat-based compost, and a mature plant only when potbound.

PROBLEMS

If the leaves turn yellow, the plant has been overwatered. Allow to dry out and water less.

If the plant becomes spindly it needs to be moved to a lighter place to encourage denser growth.

Red spider mite and aphids can attack this plant. Spray with a systemic or pyrethrum-based insecticide respectively and increase humidity.

Fatsia japonica (Japanese aralia, false castor oil plant)

EASY

An attractive evergreen shrub with dark, shiny, lobed and pointed leaves, *Fatsia japonica* will grow up to 2m/6ft as a mature houseplant and may produce creamy white flowers in autumn.

Originally from the temperate zones of Japan, where it grows in the rainforests, it is easy to look after indoors.

A quick grower, it prefers a cool spot and a protected position away from draughts, yet it is very tolerant of both high and low temperatures and can be planted outdoors in summer where it will soon acclimatize. It will not, however, withstand heavy frosts.

To encourage a denser plant, pinch out the new growth occasionally. It can also be pruned to improve its shape. Clean the leaves with a damp cloth and do not use leaf shine.

Fatsia japonica should last for many years.

PROBLEMS

If the temperature is too warm, the leaves will turn yellow and fall off. Mist and move to a cooler spot.

Overwatering will cause the leaves to droop. Allow the compost to dry out and follow the instructions in 'Water and feeding'.

Susceptible to aphids. Treat with a pyrethrum-based insecticide.

Cobwebs on the underside of leaves indicate red spider mite, encouraged by dry conditions. Water well and spray with systemic insecticide.

CARE

Light and temperature
A bright, even sunny, spot will suit this plant. The temperature should never go above 21°C/72°F in summer but can go as low as zero in winter.

Water and feeding
Immerse the pot in water for 30 minutes, drain well and allow to dry out before watering again. You may need to do this 2–3 times a week in summer, but less in winter. Mist frequently. Feed with a liquid solution at fortnightly intervals in spring and summer.

Propagation
Take basal shoots and plant in a mixture of peat and sand. Establish in a cool greenhouse or under a plastic cover in indirect light at 15°C/60°F.

Repotting
In spring, as necessary, in a no. 2 compost.

Fatsia japonica was a favourite with the Victorians, having been discovered in 1838.

Ficus benjamina 'Starlight' (Weeping fig)

EASY

This relatively recent introduction from Israel is a very much improved version of *Ficus benjamina* 'Variegata', the much sought-after tropical tree also known as the 'weeping fig'.

In good conditions 'Starlight' will grow to a densely foliaged 3m/9ft, its leaves very much whiter than the original plant and dappled with green blotches.

As a houseplant it should last for many years.

CARE

Light and temperature
Being variegated it is important that it is in a very good light situation, but away from the midday sun where the leaves could burn. It enjoys temperatures up to 24°C/75°F in summer and no lower than 13°C/55°F in winter.

Water and feeding
Water thoroughly in spring and summer, but allow the surface of the compost to dry out between waterings. Do not let the plant stand in water or the leaves will drop. During summer spray daily, particularly during high temperatures. Feed at fortnightly intervals during spring and summer with a general houseplant liquid fertilizer. In winter, depending on the temperature, 1 good watering per week should suffice.

Propagation
By stem-tip cuttings taken in spring and placed in a compost of peat and sand and maintained in a propagator at 24°C/75°F. Water the cuttings thoroughly.

Repotting
Annually in spring into a no. 2 peat-based compost. When the plant is mature, you will only need to change the topsoil in the container.

PROBLEMS

If the leaves drip, the plant is receiving insufficient light or too much water.

Brown scaly insects on the underside of the leaves will cause leaf discoloration. Remove the insects with a cloth dipped in methylated spirit.

Cobwebs on the underside of the leaves indicates red spider mite. Spray with a systemic insecticide, check watering and spray more often.

Opposite: *Ficus benjamina* 'Starlight'

F. benjamina 'Reginald'

F. benjamina 'Natasha'

F. nitida (Indian laurel) is a sun-lover and greedy for light. Its leaves are a rich dark green and the plant has an erect habit. It is used as an outdoor tub plant in the southwest of America. It does well, even in dry atmospheres.

F. 'Curly' is a colourful variety of weeping fig. Keep it in a very light position so that the leaves are well variegated.

F. longifolium likes similar conditions to *F. benjamina* but has elongated dark green leaves of up to 14cm/6in; they look dramatic displayed against white walls.

Ficus diversifolia (Mistletoe fig)

QUITE EASY

This is the hardiest and also the most slow-growing of the fig family. It grows to around 2.5m/8ft tall and has small, firm, almost round, dull green leaves which grow sparsely on a well-branched stem.

Originally from the tropical areas of India and Malaya, it produces inedible green berries which turn yellow-orange.

It is important not to overwater this plant. Mist now and again with tepid rain water and clean the leaves occasionally using a sponge.

Ficus diversifolia has a good life-expectancy as a houseplant and should live for 10–15 years.

F. diversifolia

CARE

Light and temperature
Bright but indirect light with a few hours of morning sunshine will help stimulate growth. It likes average room temperatures, but no lower than 13°C/55°F in winter.

Water and feeding
Always use tepid water for this plant. Water 2–3 times a week in summer only when the compost has dried out. Water less in winter. Feed at fortnightly intervals with a liquid solution in summer.

Propagation
From stem-tip cuttings in summer, ensuring the stems are fleshy not woody. Use a rooting hormone and provide bottom heat while the new plants are becoming established.

Repotting
Repot every 2 years, in the spring, into a loam-based no. 2 compost. For mature plants it is necessary only to change the topsoil in the pot.

PROBLEMS

Sudden loss of leaves is usually caused by overwatering or by moving the plant to a different environment.

Ficus diversifolia

Ficus elastica robusta (Indian rubber plant)

EASY

This sturdy old favourite with glossy, deep green foliage is possibly the most common houseplant of all.

Originally from the moist tropical areas of India and Malaysia, where it grows as a large tree up to 30m/90ft in height, this relatively new commercial variety is an improved version of the original, *Ficus decora.*

It is easy to grow, but is susceptible to root rot if its soil is allowed to become soggy, so take care not to overwater it.

Ficus elastica robusta can grow up to 10m/30ft indoors in a warm situation with good light. It will live to a ripe old age and can acclimatize itself to a wide range of conditions. But do remember to keep it out of dark corners and draughts.

To develop a strong, bushy plant pinch out the growing tips occasionally. The plant will 'bleed' a white sticky substance when cut, so seal the wound with petroleum jelly.

Ficus elastica robusta

CARE

Light and temperature
Bright conditions with some direct sunlight each day. It prefers a minimum temperature of 13°C/55°F throughout the year.

Water and feeding
Water thoroughly but allow the compost to dry out between waterings. Rain water is recommended since tap water may cause lime deposits on the roots which slows down the growth. Never allow the plant to stand in water for more than an hour. In winter water once a week at the most – the lower the temperature the less water is required. Feed weekly with a liquid fertilizer in spring and summer.

Propagation
Take a 7.5cm/3in length of fleshy, not woody, stem with a leaf attached. Treat it with a rooting hormone and provide bottom heat while the new plant becomes established.

Repotting
Once a year in spring in a no. 2 compost. The plant needs a large pot and probably a stake to keep it stable. For mature plants it is only necessary to change the topsoil in the pot.

PROBLEMS

If root rot occurs, indicated by leaf drop and a straggly plant, treat it immediately by completely removing the soggy compost to expose the roots. Cut away the infected roots and dust with charcoal. Repot in fresh compost.

Brown areas on the leaves mean the plant has been scorched by the sun or is too close to a heater.

Scale insect and red spider mite can attack this plant. Treat with systemic insecticide.

Ficus lyrata (Banjo fig, fiddle-leaf fig)

EASY

This imposing fig has a single stem with large, glossy, bright green violin-shaped leaves of up to 30cm/12in in length. It looks striking in a large room, though it will need to be firmly staked while growing.

Originally from the tropical rainforests of West Africa, where it grows as a close-headed tree around 12m/36ft in height, as a houseplant it will reach a substantial 6m/20ft if it has good light and warm conditions, similar to those it enjoys in its native habitat. It will withstand central heating, but does not like draughts.

The foliage must be kept dust-free and leaves should be sponged individually with tepid water. Trim the new shoots occasionally to thicken the plant. It should not need pruning except to reduce growth.

It is a sensitive plant, so if a leaf or stem is damaged or torn, cover the 'wound' with petroleum jelly or a tissue to seal it.

Ficus lyrata has been a popular houseplant since the seventies and should live for up to 12 years.

Ficus lyrata

CARE

Light and temperature
Bright but indirect light and no draughts. It likes normal room temperatures and warm conditions, but no lower than 15–18°C/60 64°F in winter.

Water and feeding
In summer immerse the pot in water for 30 minutes, drain well, and allow to dry out before watering again. In winter it will need watering less. Feed fortnightly in spring and summer with a liquid fertilizer.

Propagation
From cuttings, but this is not easy and best left to professionals.

Repotting
Each spring in a mixture of soil, peat and sand.

PROBLEMS

Drooping leaves indicate that the plant needs water. Soak well and allow to drain. It may need watering more often.

If the lower leaves turn yellow and drop, the plant has been overwatered. Allow to dry out and water less.

Brown patches may appear on the leaves, indicating that the plant needs to be moved to a warmer spot. If the brown patches become too big, snip off the leaf.

Watch for mealy bug and red spider mite. Treat with a systemic insecticide.

Ficus pumila (Creeping fig)

QUITE EASY

An elegant creeper which can also be kept in a hanging basket or trained to grow up a moss-covered pole.

Originally from the temperate areas of Indo-China and Japan, where it grows like ivy climbing over walls, *Ficus pumila* has a many-branched stem and thin, slightly crinkled, heart-shaped, dark green leaves which become larger and more oblong as the plant matures. It should grow several trails a year. There are variegated varieties, such as 'Sonny' and 'Bellis'.

This plant withstands quite cool temperatures and likes a rest period in winter at 7–10°C/44–50°F. Spray daily in summer and every second day in winter (daily if it is in a centrally heated room). This should also keep the leaves clean. Do not use leaf shine.

Ficus pumila is a long-living plant provided it is kept moist and humid, but never soggy. Cut back occasionally to encourage a dense and bushy plant.

CARE

Light and temperature
Good indirect light and a warm, shady position. In summer it will tolerate up to 30°C/84°F but the plant requires plenty of humidity at this temperature. Spray frequently. It will withstand a temperature as low as 6°C/43°F in winter as long as it is kept very much on the dry side.

Water and feeding
Water carefully, allowing the top of the compost to dry out between waterings. Never let it dry out completely, even in winter, or become soggy. Mist often. Feed every 2 weeks in spring and summer with a liquid fertilizer.

Propagation
In spring with stem-tip cuttings potted in a mixture of peat and sand. Remove lower leaves, cover with plastic and place in indirect light until new shoots appear. Repot after 4 months.

Repotting
In spring as necessary in a good house-plant mixture.

PROBLEMS

If the leaves fall off, the plant has either been allowed to dry out or its winter position is too cool and damp.

Scale insect and red spider mite may attack this plant. Spray with a systemic insecticide and improve humidity.

'Bellis'

'Sonny'

Ficus pumila

Ficus radicans 'Variegata' (Rooting fig)

QUITE DIFFICULT

This sturdy climber produces long, elegant stems with largish pointed green and creamy-white variegated leaves. It also looks good in a hanging basket.

Originally from Indonesia, where its natural habitat is the floor of the forests and lower slopes of the mountainous areas, *Ficus radicans* was first introduced as a houseplant in Victorian times.

It needs good light to maintain its leaf colour, and a humid atmosphere to do well indoors. Stand the pot over damp pebbles and spray daily in summer and every second day in winter unless it is in a centrally heated room (when it should be sprayed daily).

It is a fairly slow grower. A mature plant should have an approximate height and spread of 1m/3ft. Growing tips can be pinched out to encourage density.

It will have a long life if the conditions are sufficiently moist. Do not use leaf shine.

Ficus radicans 'Variegata'

F. radicans

PROBLEMS

If conditions are too dry the leaves will shrivel and become papery. Soak for 1 hour in a container of water, drain well, and water more often.

If the plant is overwatered or allowed to stand in water the leaves will turn yellow and fall off. Allow it almost to dry out and water more sparingly.

Scale insect can trouble this plant. Remove with a cloth dipped in methylated spirit.

Cobwebs underneath indicate red spider mite. Spray with a systemic insecticide and improve humidity.

CARE

Light and temperature
It needs bright but indirect light and fairly cool temperatures – as low as 12°C/55°F.

Water and feeding
Water 2–3 times a week in summer, never letting the compost dry out. Once a week should be sufficient in winter. Feed with a liquid fertilizer every 2 weeks when it is growing. Mist daily.

Propagation
In spring with 10cm/4in stem-tip cuttings. Place in a mixture of compost and sand and establish in a propagator or under a plastic cover at 16–18°C/61–64°F.

Repotting
For younger plants, once a year in spring in a loam- or peat-based compost. For mature plants it is necessary only to change the topsoil.

Fittonia (Snakeskin plant, mosaic plant, painted net leaf, silver net leaf)

DIFFICULT

This pretty foliage plant has delicate veined oval leaves about 7.5cm/3in long. There are two varieties: *F. argyroneura*, which has olive-green leaves with a distinct white veining, and *F. verschaffeltii*, with slightly darker green leaves and a red veining. There are also miniature versions of each. Green flowers may appear in summer and should be cut off immediately so as not to impede the plant's growth.

Originally from the tropical rainforests of Peru, where it grows as a low ground-cover creeper, it was introduced as a houseplant in the mid-nineteenth century.

Fittonia is an attractive and popular specimen that flourishes in shady situations, but it is quite difficult to grow because it needs a constant, humid temperature never below 18°C/64°F. Draughts, dry air and direct sunlight must be avoided at all costs. The plant is ideal in bottle gardens and terrariums and good in mixed bowls.

Fittonia tends to become straggly, so the new growth should be pinched out regularly to encourage density.

For the expert, this plant will have a long life.

F. verschaffeltii
(painted net leaf)

Fittonia argyroneura nana (silver net leaf)

CARE

Light and temperature
A bright to semi-shady position, but no direct sunlight. A warm temperature all year, never below 18°C/64°F.

Water and feeding
Keep the compost damp but never soggy using tepid water. Dry air will kill the plant so mist often and stand the pot over wet gravel or surround with damp peat. Feed monthly in summer with a liquid fertilizer.

Propagation
In spring using stem-tip cuttings. They will need to be established in a heated propagator at around 24°C/75°F.

Repotting
Annually in spring, in a half pot as the plant has a very shallow root system. Use a no. 2 potting compost or a no. 2 peat-based compost.

PROBLEMS

Draughts or a cold surrounding temperature will cause the leaves to drop. Move to a warmer, more protected position and improve humidity.

Dry air and direct sunlight will cause shrivelled leaves. Soak the plant in water for 30 minutes, drain well and place in a semi-shady position. Never let the compost dry out.

Yellow leaves are caused by overwatering. Remove the damaged leaves, check the drainage and allow the compost almost to dry out before watering again. Water less often.

Greenfly can attack this plant. Spray with a systemic insecticide.

Grevillea robusta (Silky oak)

EASY

This most attractive small tree has feathery, fern-like downy leaves which are silvery brown as they shoot, turning to grey-green when mature.

In the warm and temperate zones of Australia, its native habitat, it is often seen as a feature tree in gardens and along streets, growing to 30m/90ft. As a houseplant it will grow quickly to 2m/6ft.

Grevillea robusta likes to be outdoors in spring and summer, though it does well indoors if the temperature is around 18°C/64°F and the light is good. The pot should be stood over damp gravel to increase humidity.

If you would like a dense, bushy plant, pinch out the central growing shoots.

Grevillea robusta is usually past its best after 2–3 years.

Grevillea robusta will reach the ceiling given half a chance; cut back severely in late winter

PROBLEMS

Relatively problem free.

Old leaves may turn brown and should be removed. Check that the roots are not too dry.

Watch for aphids and whitefly. Spray with a pyrethrum-based insecticide.

CARE

Light and temperature
A well-lit position, quite sunny in winter, and average to warm conditions – around 18°C/64°F. In winter it can go as low as 6°C/43°F.

Water and feeding
Water once or twice a week in spring and summer, allowing the surface of the compost to dry out between waterings. In winter water less, just enough to ensure it doesn't dry out completely. Feed every 2 weeks in spring and summer with a liquid fertilizer.

Propagation
By seed in spring at a constant temperature of 13–16°C/55–61°F. It is quite difficult.

Repotting
In spring in an equal mixture of lime-free soil, peat and sand.

Gynura x. sarmentosa (Purple passion vine, velvet plant)

QUITE EASY

This unusual plant is a native of the mountainous forests of Java, where it climbs to a height of 1m/3ft, having attached itself to a tree.

For indoors it has been specially cultivated as a quick-growing perennial, producing trailing stems of up to 1.5m/4–5ft, which are also suitable for climbing.

Gynura x. sarmentosa has soft, irregularly shaped, lobed leaves that are deep red underneath and covered with a violet down. Clusters of orange flowers may appear in spring; they should be removed immediately as they have an unpleasant smell.

To maintain its colour, the plant needs direct sunlight for several hours a day, especially in winter, though in general it will tolerate average light and room temperature conditions. If the temperature is warm, stand the pot over damp gravel to ensure adequate humidity. Do not spray the foliage.

Past its best after 2 years, *Gynura* should be replaced by propagation.

CARE

Light and temperature
Several hours of sunlight each day throughout the year. In summer *Gynura* likes temperatures around 18–20°C/64–70°F and in winter between 12–14°C/53–57°F, with no lower than 10°C/50°F.

Water and feeding
Water once or twice a week, allowing the surface of the compost to dry out between waterings. If the temperature is below 15°C/59°F reduce the amount of water. Feed with a liquid solution every month all year round.

Propagation
By stem-tip cuttings of 10cm/4in, potted in a mixture of peat and sand. Stand in a well-lit position, away from direct sunlight, and when the plants are well established repot in a no. 2 loam-based compost.

Repotting
Every spring in the mixture recommended above.

PROBLEMS

If the leaves are green rather than purple, the plant needs more light.

Black marks on the leaves are caused by careless watering. Do not mist this plant and do not let water settle on the leaves.

Susceptible to greenfly, whitefly and aphids. Treat with a pyrethrum-based insecticide.

If the plant starts to look past its best, replace by propagation.

Gynura x. sarmentosa is a hybrid of *G. aurantiaca* (velvet plant) and *G. bicolor* (oak-leaved velvet plant)

Hedera helix (Common ivy, English ivy)

EASY

In ancient times ivy was the plant associated with Bacchus, the god of wine. Today there are many varieties available, but *Hedera helix* is among the most popular, as it is a quick grower and will cling easily to almost all surfaces. It also looks good in a hanging basket or as a standard.

Hedera helix grows freely in Europe, Asia and North Africa. Its lobed leaves are a glossy dark green with cream veins, growing up to 6cm/2in long.

Ivy is quite difficult to cultivate indoors because it likes a cool temperature and does not fare well in a centrally heated room. It will need frequent misting to ensure adequate humidity.

The plant will soon become straggly unless new growth is regularly pinched out. These cuttings can be propagated.

Hedera helix will have a long life, and can be moved outdoors where it will continue to grow well albeit more slowly.

CARE

Light and temperature
Bright to semi-shady conditions. Variegated plants will need light to maintain leaf colour. The temperature should be cool, ideally 15°C/60°F, and preferably unheated in winter.

Water and feeding
Do not overwater – 2–3 times a week should be sufficient in summer to keep the compost moist. In winter water less, although if it is in a heated room it will need more watering and misting. Wipe the leaves occasionally with a damp cloth. In summer feed every 2 weeks with a liquid solution.

Propagation
Easily done from stem tips or aerial roots which root easily in water or a potting mixture.

Repotting
In spring every 2 years in a good houseplant mixture. Cut the plant back at the same time to encourage bushiness.

PROBLEMS

If the plant is located in a dry position, the leaf tips will turn brown and attract spider mite and scale insect. Treat with a systemic insecticide and mist frequently to improve humidity.

If the leaf edges are brown, conditions are too warm. Cut back and move to a cooler spot.

If the veining becomes slight move to a brighter position.

Fine holes in the leaves may indicate that the plant is infested with thrips. Treat with a pyrethrum-based insecticide.

Hedera helix 'Golden Child'

Hedera helix 'Pittsburgh'

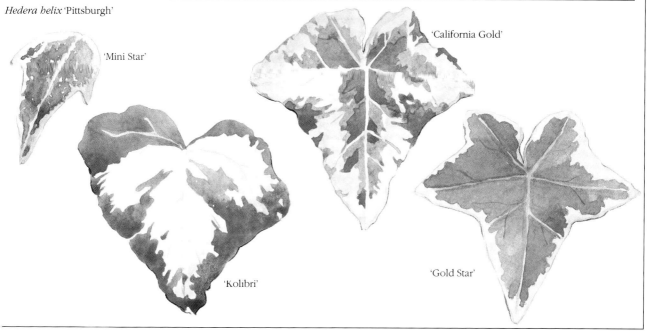

'Mini Star'

'California Gold'

'Kolibri'

'Gold Star'

Hedera canariensis (Canary Islands ivy)

EASY

This is one of the most popular varieties of ivy for the house. It is tolerant of most conditions and is easy to grow – an ideal plant for a beginner and the neglectful.

A native of the Canary Islands, where it grows freely on lower slopes, it has largish, slightly leathery, all-green leaves, but there are variegated varieties available which have silver, grey or white markings. The variety 'Gloire de Marengo' is recommended.

H. canariensis is long-lasting and a fairly quick grower that will attach itself easily to a stake, pillar or wall. It can also be grown outdoors if it is not too cold. If you do move the plant outside, do so in summer to allow it to establish itself before winter.

Pinch out the growing tips regularly to encourage a dense and bushy specimen.

Regular spraying should keep the leaves clean; if not, wipe with a damp cloth. Do not use leaf shine.

As a houseplant, it likes cool, humid conditions and will not do well if it is too hot or dry. Also take care not to overwater this plant.

CARE

Light and temperature
Bright light is essential, especially for a variegated plant. It can tolerate most temperatures, but prefers to be kept cool, the ideal being between 7–15°C/45–60°F. If the temperature is warmer, increase the humidity.

Water and feeding
Water once or twice a week in spring and summer and less in winter. Mist frequently for humidity and stand the pot over damp pebbles. In summer feed fortnightly with a liquid fertilizer.

Propagation
By stem-tip cuttings which are most easily rooted in water. Plant 2 or 3 together when established.

Repotting
Repot younger plants in spring. If the plant is growing vigorously, you may need to do this twice a year. For mature plants it is only necessary to change the topsoil.

PROBLEMS

The edges of the leaves will turn brown if the position is too dry or hot. Move to a cooler spot and improve humidity.

Black spots on the leaves mean that the plant has been overwatered. Allow to dry out and water less.

Prone to red spider mite and greenfly. Spray with a systemic insecticide and improve the humidity level.

Thrip can be sprayed with a pyrethrum-based insecticide.

Scale insect will discolour the leaves. Remove with a cloth dipped in methylated spirit.

Hedera canariensis 'Gloire de Marengo' has been cultivated in Europe for over 200 years

Howea (Paradise palm, kentia palm, sentry palm)

QUITE DIFFICULT

This palm is native to Lord Howe Island off the east coast of Australia, where it lives in subtropical, seaside conditions. It has only recently become a sought-after houseplant.

The differences between the two species – *H. forsteriana* (paradise palm or kentia palm) and *H. belmoreana* (sentry palm) – are sometimes hard to distinguish. In its native habitat, *H. forsteriana* will grow up to 20m/60ft, its fronds well spaced and durable. *H. belmoreana* is more slow-growing and its fronds are thinner and more upright.

Both varieties have a single, robust trunk from which grow dark green pinnate fronds which should be cleaned regularly with a damp cloth. The plants may also produce clusters of yellow-green fruit.

Avoid direct sunlight which will turn the leaf tips brown. *Howea* can withstand almost completely shady conditions, but the plant will not grow unless there is some light. Good drainage is essential.

Howea is extremely long-lasting – up to 80 years.

CARE

Light and temperature
Light to semi-shady conditions, always avoiding direct sunlight. Average to warm temperatures throughout the year, and no lower than 10°C/50°F in winter.

Water and feeding
Water well in spring and summer, and always keep the compost moist. In winter it will need watering less often. Avoid saturation and never allow the compost to dry out. Mist often. Feed fortnightly in spring and summer with a general houseplant fertilizer.

Propagation
From seed in a propagator at 27°C/80°F. This is difficult to do, and best left to professionals.

Repotting
Only when potbound as the plant does not like to be disturbed. Use a good soil- and peat-based mixture.

PROBLEMS

Howea adapts well as a houseplant as long as it has a warm, humid and protected spot and is neither overwatered nor underwatered.

Overwatering will make the leaves turn brown. Allow to dry out and water less.

Underwatering will make the leaves turn yellow. Immerse the pot in water for 30 minutes, drain well, and never allow the compost to dry out.

The lower leaves will die naturally, and should be cut off.

Red spider mite will attack the plant if conditions are too dry. Spray with a systemic insecticide and improve humidity.

Howea forsteriana

Hypoestes sanguinolenta (Polka dot plant, freckle face)

QUITE DIFFICULT

Clockwise from the top: *H. s.* 'Bettina', *H. s.* 'Rose', *H. s.* 'White', *H. s.* 'Ruby'

CARE

Light and temperature
It likes bright, indirect sunlight, with plenty of warmth and humidity. Place the pot over damp pebbles and maintain a temperature of 18–24°C/64–75°F all year round if possible.

Water and feeding
Water 2–3 times a week in summer, and possibly only once a week in winter using tepid water. Feed with half the recommended dose of liquid fertilizer at fortnightly intervals.

Propagation
It is best to raise a new plant from seed each spring. Cuttings can also be rooted in spring and summer in a mixture of soil, peat and sand. Either place them in a propagator or cover the pot with plastic and keep at a constant temperature of not less than 21°C/70°F while they become established.

Repotting
If growing fast, pot on during the first season. Discard when plant becomes leggy.

A showy houseplant originating from Madagascar, where it grows in humid, tropical conditions as a ground-cover plant. It has small, downy, oblong green leaves with coloured veins and splashes of pink spots. New varieties have been bred to include white, ruby and rose colourings and these are much more compact in habit. There are often several plants in a small pot.

Hypoestes is a very good ground-cover plant for mixed bowls and bottle gardens, but it needs adequate light to keep its colouring bright and vibrant. It also tends to become very straggly and it is best to replace it annually. Pinch out the growing tips in young plants.

This plant is quite particular about its position. Do not put it in a dry atmosphere or near a heater or gas fire. Do not use leaf shine.

PROBLEMS

This plant is sensitive to the cold and to being overwatered in winter, causing it to droop. Allow the soil to dry out in a warmer position and then water less.

Discoloured leaves indicate the plant has been attacked by scale insect. Remove these with a cloth dipped in methylated spirit.

Leea coccinea

QUITE DIFFICULT

This striking shrub-like plant is grown for its most attractive burgundy-coloured, multi-pointed leaves, which will turn green as the plant matures. It may produce small grape-like flowers.

Originally a low-growing shrub from the dense tropical forests of Cambodia, it was introduced into England during the 1880s and owes its name to the famous Scottish gardener James Lee. It is now enjoying a revival in popularity – and deservedly so.

Indoors it requires a high level of humidity and moisture and a warm temperature all year round, but will not tolerate draughts. It should last for 5–6 years.

A healthy plant will produce droplets on the leaves, which is natural.

L. c. 'Burgundy' will only keep its red colour in good light

Leea coccinea 'Green'

CARE

Light and temperature
Bright but indirect light is necessary to maintain the colour of its foliage. It likes warm temperatures all year, preferably no lower than 16°C/61°F in winter.

Water and feeding
Keep quite moist at all times, but never soggy. The compost must not be allowed to dry out. Provide plenty of humidity and mist often. Feed with a weak solution every 2 weeks in spring and summer.

Propagation
From seed or stem cuttings in a warm propagator. This is difficult and best left to a professional.

Repotting
In spring, as necessary, in a good houseplant mixture, ensuring adequate drainage.

PROBLEMS

If the air is too dry the plant will be attacked by aphids and red spider mite. Spray aphids with a pyrethrum-based insecticide and remove spider mites with a cloth dipped in methylated spirit.

Leea is sensitive to overwatering and underwatering, both of which will cause the leaves to drop. Follow the instructions in 'Water and feeding' carefully.

Licuala grandis

QUITE EASY

A native of the New Britain
Islands near New Guinea, this
very attractive small fan palm has
a slim trunk, around 2m/6ft tall,
topped with almost round green
leaves that are plaited and
toothed along the edge.

Recently commercialized
species are available from 60cm/
24in, though you will need to
hunt for them as production is
relatively small.

Licuala grandis

CARE

Light and temperature
Diffused sunlight, but will take quite low
light conditions. The plant must be kept
warm all year round with a minimum
temperature of 15°C/60°F. It loves warmth
and will take temperatures up to 30°C/
85°F.

Water and feeding
Being a stove plant it enjoys high humidity.
During spring and summer place on a
saucer of wet pebbles. Water thoroughly,
but do not allow it to stand in water and
become waterlogged. Spray leaves daily
when the temperature rises above 18°C/
64°F. During winter water weekly but do
not allow the soil to dry out. Feed with
general houseplant fertilizer at fortnightly
intervals during spring and summer.

Propagation
Difficult. Best left to a professional.

Repotting
In spring, but only if rootbound, in a no.2
loam-based compost.

PROBLEMS

Webs on the underside of leaves indicate
red spider mite, caused by the plant
becoming too dry. Spray with diluted
malathion at fortnightly intervals. Raise
humidity and water the plant thoroughly.

Maranta leuconeura (Prayer plant, rabbit's tracks, red herringbone plant)

QUITE DIFFICULT

M. l. 'Kerchoveana' and *M. l.* 'Erythrophylla' (also known as *M. tricolor*) are two of the most popular varieties of this family of plants renowned for its beautiful leaf markings, some almost appearing as if they are hand-painted.

Both are known as prayer plants as their leaves curl up at night.

Maranta is quite a difficult houseplant to maintain because of its humidity requirements, but worth persevering with. It should last for many years, but it is usually best to divide the plant after 3 or 4 years.

Originally from the tropical rainforests of South America, where it grows as a small plant with spreading branches under the protection of the tree canopy, *Maranta* likes warm conditions with plenty of humidity. Use soft and tepid water at all times. Spray daily and stand the pot on wet pebbles or surround with moist peat to ensure good humidity. If spraying doesn't keep the leaves clean, wipe gently with a damp cloth. Do not use leaf shine.

'Amabilis'

'Freddy'

M. ornata

CARE

Light and temperature
Bright light but never direct sun. It likes warm temperatures, ideally 16–18°C/60–64°F all year, and as high as 28°C/83°F if there is good humidity. Avoid draughts.

Water and feeding
Keep the compost moist at all times with tepid water, never allowing it to dry out between waterings. It will need less water in winter. Mist leaves regularly. Feed every 2 weeks in late spring and early summer with a weak liquid solution.

Propagation
Divide the plant in early spring as new growth emerges, ensuring each division has both roots and stems, and transfer to individual 9cm/4in pots. Cover with plastic and keep warm – 18°C/64°F – until established.

Repotting
In spring every 2–3 years in a peat-based compost. Ensure adequate drainage.

PROBLEMS

This is a delicate plant. Falling leaves or brown leaf tips may be caused by the air being too dry. Remove dead growth and improve the humidity. Also check for red spider mite and remove with a cloth dipped in methylated spirit.

Underwatering is indicated by curled or spotted leaves and yellow lower leaves. Remove the damaged leaves and keep the compost moist at all times.

Maranta leuconeura 'Erythrophylla'

Peperomia caperata

EASY

There are several hundred members of this small, bushy, herbaceous family which is characterized by a great variety of attractive and unusual leaves and colours.

Originally from tropical areas of Brazil, where it is found under the tree canopy, *Peperomia* grows to 10–15cm/4–6in high and often produces creamy white flower spikes. It also looks good in a hanging basket.

It likes warm, humid conditions, as in its native habitat, with bright but indirect sunlight. Spray the foliage daily and stand the pot over damp gravel to ensure adequate humidity.

This plant is past its best after 2–3 years when it becomes quite straggly. It can then be propagated.

PROBLEMS

Overwatering will cause leaf and stem rot, particularly in winter. Allow the compost almost to dry out between waterings.

Dry air will cause the leaves to turn brown and fall. Improve humidity by standing the pot over damp gravel and misting frequently.

Red spider mite will cause the leaves to go yellow with cobwebbing on the underside. Spray with systemic insecticide.

CARE

Light and temperature
Bright to semi-shady conditions with a temperature of around 21°C/70°F. It will tolerate temperatures as low as 10°C/50°F in winter if the compost is kept fairly dry.

Water and feeding
Keep moist all year round, but do not allow the compost to get soggy, especially in winter, or the roots and stem will rot. Ensure good humidity all year. Feed at monthly intervals in summer with a liquid solution.

Propagation
In spring or summer with leaf bud or stem cuttings into a good houseplant mixture.

Repotting
Only when potbound, in a soil-based compost.

Peperomia caperata 'Emerald Ripple' one of the small-leaved species

Peperomia caperata 'Nigra' and 'Lilium'

P. caperata
'Pixie Variegata'

P. caperata 'Helios'

P. caperata
'Variegata' (or
variegated ripple)

P. glabella 'Variegata'
(or variegated wax
privet) has tiny leaves
on attractive red stems

P. clusifolia, commonly
known as the red-edged
peperomia

Radermachera (Emerald tree, Asian bell tree)

EASY

This is a recently introduced houseplant which has become popular because of its attractive appearance and resistance to the dry atmosphere of most homes.

A native of China and Taiwan, where it grows as a tiny evergreen tree, it has small, shiny, veined leaves with long points. As a houseplant it has the appearance of a small tree and may produce yellow bells.

Although quite easy to look after, *Radermachera* will not do well near fires or smokers, as smoke will cause it to lose its leaves.

Radermachera needs bright conditions with plenty of humidity, so spray often. The plant also benefits from a spell outdoors in summer in a protected spot.

It should last for several years.

CARE

Light and temperature
Bright indirect light and average room temperatures all year, no lower than 15°C/60°F in winter.

Water and feeding
Water regularly to keep the compost moist at all times. In winter water more sparingly. Avoid sogginess, but never let the compost dry out. Feed each week in spring and summer with a liquid fertilizer.

Propagation
In summer by stem cuttings. Establish in a propagator at a temperature of 21°C/71°F.

Repotting
As necessary, in spring, in a no. 2 peat-based compost.

PROBLEMS

Dry or overly warm conditions in winter may cause the plant to be attacked by red spider mite or scale insect. Remove with a cloth dipped in methylated spirit.

Susceptible to aphids and thrips. Spray with a pyrethrum-based insecticide.

Radermachera

Raphis (Lady palm)

EASY

One of the most popular palms in America, there are many varieties of *Raphis*, which has delicate heads of fan-shaped leaves topping thin stems of unbranching 'bamboo'. Like many of the palms, *Raphis* comes from Southern China, where it grows in the tropical and shady rainforests, receiving little or no sunlight. It was introduced into Europe in the 1890s.

There are dwarf varieties available, growing to 60cm/2ft, and also varieties with variegated leaves that can occasionally be found for sale as indoor plants. The most commonly available are *Raphis excelsa*, which reaches 2m/80cm, and the somewhat smaller, more delicate, *Raphis humilis*.

The lady palm likes good air circulation and can look very decorative in a stairwell during the winter months, appreciating a spell on a warm patio outside in summer, providing it receives little sun. It makes an excellent conservatory plant.

Raphis excelsa can be bought in dwarf forms which have variegated leaves

CARE

Light and temperature
A semi-sunny location and good light. It will cope with cooler temperatures, 10°C/50°F in winter and average temperatures in summer. Avoid temperature fluctuations and draughts.

Water and feeding
Keep the compost evenly moist, watering freely in summer and less so in winter. It needs good humidity and the palmate fronds should be misted regularly. In summer feed every 7 days with a weak solution of liquid fertilizer.

Propagation
Shoots can be carefully separated from the main plant and potted up into loam-based compost. Nursery men propagate from seed at high temperatures, but as a houseplant *Raphis* will not flower or produce seed.

Repotting
Necessary only when the plant outgrows its pot. Use well-draining loam-based soil and move to a pot one size larger in spring.

PROBLEMS

Red spider mite can attack this plant. Spray with a systemic insecticide.

If the leaf tips of the fronds become brown, move the plant to a slightly cooler position and increase the humidity. Stand on a tray of pebbles.

Selaginella martensii (Resurrection plant, rose of Jericho)

QUITE EASY

This pretty compact plant has fleshy light green feathery leaves which hang down in rows from small upright stems. As a houseplant it will grow to approximately 30cm/1ft high with a spread of 15cm/6in.

Its native habitat, among the undergrowth of the mountainous forests of Mexico, is damp and protected, and indoors it needs similar conditions – moderately warm and shady with good humidity. It is ideal for a terrarium. Spray daily and stand the pot over damp gravel. Avoid dry and draughty conditions and do not use leaf shine.

It should last for 2–3 years.

'Variegata'

PROBLEMS

If conditions are too dry, the leaves will turn yellow and die. Cut off the affected ones, submerge the pot in water for a short time and drain well. Mist frequently.

Susceptible to aphids and red spider mite. Spray aphids with a pyrethrum-based insecticide and mites with a systemic insecticide.

CARE

Light and temperature
Shady or indirect light and warm temperatures, preferably 18–24°C/64–75°F in summer, down to 12°C/55°F in winter.

Water and feeding
Water well all year, keeping the compost moist but not soggy. Spray with tepid water every day. Use a weak liquid fertilizer every 3 weeks in spring and summer.

Propagation
In spring by taking 7.5cm/3in cuttings and planting in a moist no. 2 peat-based compost. Keep warm and in indirect light. It will not take long to establish and can then be planted in another pot.

Repotting
Every spring, in the same pot, in a mixture of no. 2 peat-based compost

Selaginella martensii is one of the more erect forms

Senecio rowleyanus (String of pearls)

QUITE EASY

This trailing plant with succulent pea-like leaves hails from Southern Namibia where it can be found growing from the rocky outcrops in full sun. The plant will form dense mats.

It is best used in a hanging basket, either indoors or in a good sunny situation in a conservatory. There the beadlike leaves, which are marbled in greens and whites, can be seen to good advantage.

The common name of the plant is obvious once it is seen.

Good air circulation is important as these plants have been adapted from a naturally airy growing site.

Senecio rowleyanus

CARE

Light and temperature
In summer in a sunny position. It will withstand a temperature up to 30°C/85°F. In winter keep in good light but the temperature may go down to 10°C/50°F.

Water and feeding
Allow the surface of the compost to dry out between waterings. Feed at monthly intervals during spring and summer with a general houseplant fertilizer at half strength.

Propagation
Break off 10cm/4in pieces of stem, allow to dry for 48 hours and pot into cactus compost at a temperature of 21°C/71°F.

Repotting
Every second year in a cactus compost.

PROBLEMS

Aphids may attack this plant. Spray with a systemic insecticide.

Syngonium (Goosefoot plant)

QUITE EASY

Syngonium 'White Butterfly'

CARE

Light and temperature
Bright but indirect light and temperatures around 17–21°C/64–70°F are ideal. In winter the temperature should not go below 15°C/60°F.

Water and feeding
In spring and summer do not let the plant dry out, so water 3–4 times a week. Stand the plant on pebbles almost covered with water to provide good humidity, which the plant thrives upon. Feed every 2 weeks with a general houseplant fertilizer. In winter water less and allow the plant to dry out between waterings.

Propagation
Take stem-tip cuttings approximately 10cm/4in in length. Dip them in a rooting hormone and place in a cutting compost in a propagator at 21°C/70°F.

Repotting
Each spring in a peat-based compost.

PROBLEMS

Scale insect and red spider mite trouble this plant. Remove scale insect with a cloth dipped in methylated spirit and spider mite with a systemic insecticide.

If the plant becomes straggly, it needs more light.

There are several commercial varieties of this plant available, but the most popular is 'White Butterfly', which has large white leaves with green edges. An unusual feature of *Syngonium* is the changing shape of its leaves, which are oval, becoming lobed as they mature.

This pretty climber from Central America can be found growing in trees, using its aerial roots to cling on to whatever it is climbing. Indoors, it will do well if it is trained up a damp moss pole, from which it will also gather moisture. A vigorous grower, it needs repotting often.

As in its native habitat, it needs a good humidity level, so mist frequently and place the pot over damp gravel. There it has beautiful white flowers but these do not appear in the pot plant.

As a houseplant it will grow up to 1.5m/4–5ft and should last for several years, at which point it can easily be propagated.

Syngonium is often sold under the name *Nephthytis.*

Tolmiea menziesii (Piggyback plant)

EASY

This perennial herb, with soft green heart-shaped leaves covered with white bristles, grows identical miniature plants which can be cut off and rooted. In spring it may also produce small greenish flowers.

It was originally from the warm temperate Pacific coast of America where it grows as far north as Alaska. It is good for hanging baskets or as a ground cover and will reach an average height of 15cm/6in with a spread of 30cm/1ft.

It is easy to grow indoors because it likes a cool, well-ventilated spot out of the sun. Avoid warm, dry air. Mist the leaves occasionally and do not let the compost dry out. Do not use leaf shine.

After 2–3 years it can become straggly so it is best to propagate. It can eventually be planted outdoors.

CARE

Light and temperature
A bright to semi-shady, well-ventilated position. In summer it does well outdoors; indoors keep the temperature around 18°C/64°F. In winter it likes a cool position, between 5–10°C/40–50°F. An unheated room is ideal, but ensure it has good light.

Water and feeding
Water 2–3 times a week in spring and summer. In winter it will need less water –
just enough to keep the compost moist. Feed at fortnightly intervals in spring and summer with a weak liquid fertilizer.

Propagation
Easily done by taking an offshoot and planting it in a soil- or peat-based compost.

Repotting
Repot annually in spring using a soil- or peat-based compost.

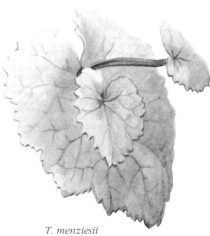

T. menziesii

PROBLEMS

Direct sunlight can damage the leaves. Make sure the plant is in a bright position, away from the sun.

If the leaves turn brown the plant is too hot and should be moved to a cooler position.

Overwatering and a cold temperature may cause stem rot, which can be recognized by brown slimy marks on the stem. Move to a warmer position and allow the compost to dry out. Water more sparingly, especially in winter.

Red spider mite can attack this plant. Spray with a systemic insecticide.

Tolmiea menziesii is very hardy

Tradescantia (Wandering Jew, inch plant)

EASY

Originally from Central America, Argentina and Brazil, this energetic creeper has smallish, shiny, oval green leaves with creamy yellow stripes and banks. In its native habitat it is found as a ground-cover and trailing plant. Its fast-growing stems, with their profusion of leaves, make it ideal for a hanging basket. New growth can be pinched out to encourage a denser plant.

Tradescantia is a good plant for the beginner as it accommodates a reasonable range of conditions and will not die if it misses out on the occasional watering. Its only disadvantage is that it tends to become straggly after a year or two and should be replaced by propagation, which is very easy.

It only needs to be misted occasionally, which should keep the leaves sufficiently clean.

From the same group as *Tradescantia* is the species *Zebrina*, which comes from Mexico. Strong direct light intensifies its leaf colours.

CARE

Light and temperature
Bright but indirect light, especially for variegated varieties, which need light to maintain their leaf colour. The ideal temperature is 18°C/64°F all year.

Water and feeding
Water 2–3 times a week in spring and summer and once a week in winter, allowing the soil almost to dry out between waterings. Mist occasionally. Fertilize every 2 weeks in spring and summer with a general houseplant solution.

Propagation
It is best to propagate each year in spring. Stem-tip cuttings will root easily in a mixture of loam and sand or in water, and have no special temperature requirements.

Repotting
Propagation is recommended.

PROBLEMS

If the leaves turn brown, the plant is either too dry or in too much light. Water more frequently and make sure it does not have direct sunlight.

Straggly growth means that the plant needs lighter conditions or that it is past its best and should be replaced by propagation.

Red spider mite and greenfly tend to attack this plant. Spray spider mite with a systemic insecticide and greenfly with a pyrethrum-based insecticide.

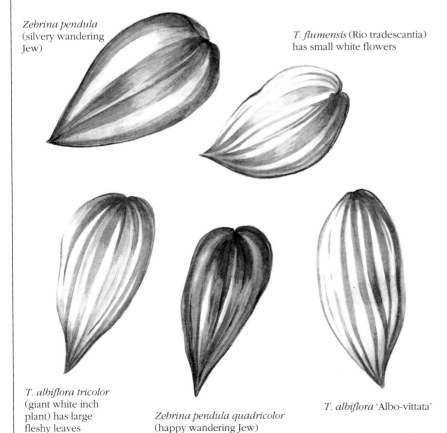

Zebrina pendula
(silvery wandering Jew)

T. flumensis (Rio tradescantia) has small white flowers

T. albiflora tricolor
(giant white inch plant) has large fleshy leaves

Zebrina pendula quadricolor
(happy wandering Jew)

T. albiflora 'Albo-vittata'

Opposite: *Tradescantia*

Yucca elephantipes (Spineless yucca, pine lily)

EASY

This most exotic member of the lily family comes from the subtropical areas of Mexico and Guatemala, where it grows to a height of 15m/45ft in sunny, arid conditions.

The sturdy trunk is swollen at the base and from the top grow numerous rosettes of firm, glossy green, pointed leaves. It can also produce clusters of creamy white flowers.

Canes of 30cm–2m/1–6ft are now imported from the West Indies and Central America and quite often different stem lengths are potted together.

As a houseplant *Yucca elephantipes* is hardy and not at all temperamental, preferring a dry, sunny position, but also able to adapt to semi-shade. Mist occasionally. Wipe the leaves with a damp cloth from time to time but do not use leaf shine. The plant will benefit from a spell outdoors in summer.

It should live for many years.

Yucca elephantipes flowers after a number of years

CARE

Light and temperature
Bright light, even direct sunlight, especially in winter, though it will also be happy in a semi-shady position. It likes a temperature of 18–22°C/64–71°F all year, and no lower than 7°C/45°F in winter.

Water and feeding
Water thoroughly, but allow the compost almost to dry out between waterings. It will need less water in winter. Spray occasionally. Feed at fortnightly intervals in spring and summer.

Propagation
Side shoots will appear in spring that can be planted on individually in small pots in a mixture of no. 2 compost and sand. Maintain a constant temperature of 24°C/75°F until established.

Repotting
For young plants, repot every second year in a no. 2 compost mixed with sand. For mature plants it is necessary only to change the topsoil.

PROBLEMS

If the leaves turn yellow, the plant probably needs more light. Cut off the damaged leaves and move to a sunnier position.

Scale insect can attack this plant. Spray with a systemic insecticide.

Bromeliads

The glorious leaf colours of bromeliads are unforgettable and dramatic; they are showy plants and well worth having for the sharp colours of their flowers alone. Imagine a South American jungle filled with orchids and bromeliads, in all their brilliant colours, on the floor of the forest and attached to the trunks of trees.

There are over 1400 known species of bromeliad; in this book we have covered some of those most adaptable to cultivation as indoor plants. They should be watered through the natural well in the centre of the plant for, in their native habitat, the rain falls on the leaves and runs down into this well.

The mother plant of the bromeliad dies after flowering, leaving behind it 2 or 3 plantlets to grow on and replace it. Plants should ideally be purchased when the flower spathe is just beginning to emerge from the well.

Aechmea fasciata (Urn plant, Greek vase plant, bottle brush plant)

EASY

This plant, also known as *Billbergia rhodocynea*, comes from Brazil, where it was discovered in 1826. Naturally epiphytic, its natural habitat is on the floor of the jungle.

The name *Aechmea* derives from the Greek for lance tip – a reference to the sharply pointed central pink bract that is surrounded by long strap-shaped leaves. The actual flowers are small and blue, blooming on the edges of the spike in summer and lasting for up to 6 weeks. The plant forms a natural well that holds water in its centre.

After the flowers die, the pink spike slowly shrivels and at the same time replaces itself with 2 or 3 baby spikes or rosettes. Eventually these baby spikes can be repotted as individual plants, but the main plant will not bloom again for another year.

Aechmea will grow to 60cm/2ft across with leaves up to 30cm/1ft long. It will be 3 or 4 years old before the pink bract spikes appear and the plant flowers for the first time. There is a very striking variety called 'Purpurea' that has maroon-coloured leaves with silver markings.

CARE

Light and temperature
Aechmea is a very tolerant plant and can take either direct or indirect sunlight. The temperature should be no lower than 12°C/55°F and no higher than 27°C/80°F.

Water and feeding
Water twice a week and keep 2.5cm/½in water in the central spike. If possible, use rain water. Do not feed. Misting the leaves with weak solutions of fertilizer helps.

Propagation
The amateur finds offsets easier than raising seed. In springtime remove the offsets at the base of the plant once they look to be viable (after 4–6 months). Pot them on into a rich, barely moist potting compost. Do not separate the new rosette until the parent has completely shrivelled up.

Repotting
This is rarely required, but if needs be should be done at the onset of the growing period.

PROBLEMS

The flower stem may rot through overwatering at too low temperatures. Empty the rosette and allow the compost to dry out.

If the leaves develop brown tips and shrivel before flowering, the plant is getting too hot and dry. Increase watering.

If greenfly infests the plant, spray with diluted malathion.

Aechmea is also prone to scale insect and mealy bug, which should be treated with methylated spirit.

If bract spikes and flowers fail to appear move the plant to a sunnier situation.

Aechmea fasciata

Guzmania lingulata major (Scarlet star)

EASY

Guzmania lingulata 'Empire'

'Orangeade'

This is a striking houseplant, with strappy green leaves and a bright red or orange star-shaped bract that produces small white or yellow flowers, which soon fade away.

There are almost 90 species of *Guzmania*, their native habitat the West Indies and South America. The plant is named after the Spanish chemist, Antonino Guzman, and was introduced into Europe at the beginning of the nineteenth century. It grows naturally on the forest floor under deep-shade leaf canopy.

Although it is an epiphyte, in the house it is usually grown in a pot, but can do well if tied on to pieces of bark with its roots bound into sphagnum moss.

Guzmania dies after it has produced its flowers in summer but a new plant can easily be propagated from the offsets which appear as the parent plant dies.

It can grow to 30–38cm/12–15in tall and 25cm/10in across with a life expectancy of 2–3 years.

New hybrids are constantly being introduced by nursery men. *G. lingulata major* from Ecuador does well with its scarlet star, and *G. l.* 'Orangeade' and *G. l.* 'Empire' are just two of the dramatic new plants now available.

CARE

Light and temperature
A bright situation, but protect the plant from strong direct sun in the middle of the day. Keep between 15–18°C/60–64°F in summer and ensure the humidity level is high.

Water and feeding
Water up to 3 times weekly, keeping the potting compost moist. In winter, water only once a week. Do not feed. If possible, spray with rain water and keep about 2.5cm/1in water in the central funnel of the bract. Refill this every 3 weeks or so.

Propagation
The young shoots, which should be 9cm/3in long, appear as the parent plant is in flower. Wait until these offshoots have roots of their own before separating them, preferably in spring. Then use potting soil suitable for orchids.

Repotting
Not necessary.

PROBLEMS

If the lower leaves go brown, water the plant more often. It is normal for bromeliads to die back after flowering, but new offshoots will appear.

Rot at the base of the plant may have been caused by overwatering. Reduce watering immediately. The plant may well not recover.

Neoregelia carolinae (Blushing bromeliad, cartwheel plant)

EASY

This is one of the most spectacular bromeliads. It has stiff strap-shaped leaves, which turn a brilliant red colour near the centre of the plant, usually in spring towards flowering time.

The plant has a central funnel with small purple summer flowers, which are far less dramatic than the surrounding red leaves. *Neoregelia carolinae* 'Tricolor' is an even more striking variety, as it has yellow striped leaves as well as the central red ones.

This plant can grow to a span of 60cm/2ft, but is more often only 38–46cm/15–18in across.

As an indoor plant it can live for up to 5 years.

Neoregelia carolinae 'Marechalli'. Its red centre can spread to over half the plant.

CARE

Light and temperature
Strong light, which enhances the colour of the foliage, is needed, but avoid scorching midday sun, as the symmetry of the plant is ruined by the removal of sun-scorched leaves. Keep temperatures at 15°C/60°F all year, never below 13°C/55°F in winter or above 21°C/70°F in summer.

Water and feeding
Keep the central funnel full of water at all times, as this is from where the plant draws most of its nourishment. About once a month, drain the cup and refill with fresh water. In summer, water the compost as well, once or twice a week, always keeping it moist. Feed each fortnight in summer with a half-strength dose of liquid food.

Propagation
After flowering, the mother plant produces plantlets. Wait for them to grow to half the size of the parent; then cut free and plant into a sandy compost containing perlite. Keep humidity high and pot on after 3 months into 12cm/5in pots filled with a good draining and light compost, including grit and charcoal if possible.

Repotting
Each May, into a pot one size larger.

PROBLEMS

If the leaves lose their glorious colour, put the plant on a window ledge where its foliage will brighten up quickly. But beware of leaves becoming scorched.

Brown leaf tips may be caused by allowing the compost to dry out. Water frequently, particularly in summer months.

If the leaves become motley, check the lime content in the water as lime deposits can cause stain marks.

Nidularium (Bird's nest)

EASY

This bromeliad, from tropical South America, is rarely seen. Like the *Neoregelia*, it has a central rosette of very short leaves. This 'bird's nest' turns bright red in summer during flowering time – the plant's name derives from the Latin word *nidus*, meaning nest. The stiff strappy leaves can grow to about 30cm/12in long. The white flowers are uninteresting and short-lived.

There are many varieties of this plant. *N. innocentii* has saw-edged leaves which are coloured purple above and wine-red underneath. *N innocentii striatum* has variegated leaves while *N. fulgens* (blushing cap) has spotted ones.

Nidularium innocentii

CARE

Light and temperature
Bright light, but away from direct midday sun. Again keep temperatures at about 15°C/60°F all year round.

Water and feeding
Ensure the central funnel is full of water at all times. During the summer months, keep the compost moist by watering once or twice a week. It requires high humidity so place it on a tray of wet pebbles.

Propagation
By offsets, which appear at the base of the plant. Wait until the mother plant has shrivelled completely after flowering, then separate the rosettes and pot them on into a sandy, well-draining compost. Keep them moist, at temperatures of 15°C/60°F.

Repotting
Only when separating plantlets or when seriously pot bound.

PROBLEMS

Overwatering will cause the plant to rot and die. Water the compost less often.

If the leaves develop brown tips, either the air is too dry or the plant is receiving insufficient water. Increase watering, using rain water if possible, and mist during summer.

Tillandsia lindenii (Blue-flowered torch)

EASY

This dramatic bromeliad has grass-like leaves and an eye-catching central pink bract with a flower head up to 30cm/12in long. The bracts bear deep blue flowers with white throats 5cm/2in across.

Like all bromeliads, its native habitat is in the tropical and subtropical areas of South America and it is an epiphyte, growing on rocks or on the trunks and in hollows of other trees and plants, which give it support. The plant can also thrive in arid desert.

Tillandsia cyanea (pink quill) has similar leaves but a more compact and smaller flower head, which is again coloured pink with plain blue flowers.

Both *Tillandsia cyanea* and *Tillandsia lindenii* are green-leaved bromeliads.

The tillandsias sold as pot plants are often either attached to a stone or growing from the branch of a tree. They have practically no roots, and feed and nourish themselves through their leaves. *Tillandsia usneoides* (air plant or Spanish moss) is the most commonly purchased of the grey tillandsias.

CARE

Light and temperature
Bright filtered light suits *Tillandsia*, but keep it away from direct midday sun. Average room temperatures should be maintained throughout the year.

Water and feeding
Keep the central funnel full of water at all times. As well, during the summer, keep the compost moist by watering once or twice a week. The plant should be stood on a tray of damp pebbles to increase humidity. Mist the leaves frequently. Do not feed.

Propagation
By offshoots which appear at the base of the plant as the spike starts to die back. Wait until the mother plant has completely shrivelled up after flowering before separating and potting on the new plantlets. Use a bromeliad soil or sandy compost. Keep moist, at a temperature of 15°C/60°F.

Repotting
Only when absolutely necessary.

PROBLEMS

If the flowers fail to appear in spring, move the plant to a lighter position.

Insufficient water or dry atmospheres can cause the leaf tips to brown. Increase watering, using rain water if possible, and mist the leaves often.

Rot can be caused by overwatering.

Opposite: *Tillandsia cyanea*

Vriesea splendens (Flame sword)

DIFFICULT

There are around 100 known species of *Vriesea*, one of the showiest of the bromeliads. It is named after the Dutch botanist, W. H. de Vriese and is a native of tropical Guyana.

V. splendens 'Major' is the most readily available variety. It has stiff strappy dark green leaves, with purple- or chocolate-coloured bands running across them, which grow up to 45cm/18in long.

The central bright orange bract gives the plant its common name of flaming sword. It may appear at anytime throughout the year and can last for months. In summer small yellow flowers develop, but only after the plant has been potted up for several years.

CARE

Light and temperature
3–4 hours a day of direct sunlight will force the bromeliad into flower. Hot midday sun should be avoided. Keep the temperature at around 15°C/60°F throughout the year.

Water and feeding
As for all bromeliads, liquid fertilizer should not be given. Keep the potting compost moist by watering once or twice a week in summer months and less frequently during the cooler times. Mist the leaves and stand the plant on a tray of moist pebbles to increase humidity.

Propagation
Offsets are formed in spring and can be separated from the parent plant after the plant spike has shrivelled completely. They should be cut away with a sharp knife and potted on into a well-drained sandy compost. Keep the temperature on the warm side and avoid draughts.

Repotting
Only when absolutely essential, if the plant is potbound.

PROBLEMS

Overwatering can cause the plant to rot. It will be difficult to rescue, but try cutting down on watering immediately.

If the bract spikes do not appear, move the plant to a sunnier situation in early spring.

If the atmosphere is too dry brown tips may develop at the end of the leaves. Increase humidity by placing the plant on a tray of moist pebbles.

The spathe of *Vriesea splendens* 'Major' should be removed after the flowers die

Ferns

Among the oldest plants known, there are some 250 species of fern found all over the world. They were fashionable in Victorian times and today their delicate and attractive leaves make them popular as indoor plants, particularly in mixed groupings.

Ferns reproduce themselves through spores and do not flower. Many of them grow naturally in deep shade in tropical forests; others are epiphytic, found attached high up on tree trunks or colonizing cliff tops in full sunshine. They are mostly rhizomes.

As indoor plants, all ferns will do well if given high humidity. Standing the plant on a tray of damp pebbles is essential for success, but plants do not like spray-misting on their leaves.

Asparagus falcatus (Sicklethorn)

EASY

This showy, fern-like plant is actually a member of the lily family. It comes from South Africa, where it grows in protected and shady subtropical conditions.

It is a tolerant plant, with sturdy prickly stems from which grow delicate needle-shaped leaves. It will sometimes produce white flowers and then attractive but poisonous red berries.

Asparagus falcatus is not particularly fussy about its conditions, except it will not do well in temperatures above 21°C/ 70°F. The fronds will gradually die and should be cut off when they are past their best.

The plant will usually live for 3 years, after which time it should be propagated from seed.

Do not use leaf shine.

CARE

Light and temperature
Quite cool and shady conditions away from bright light. In summer the ideal temperature is 12–15°C/55–60°F. In winter it can go as low as 8°C/45°F.

Water and feeding
In summer water 2–3 times a week, never allowing the compost to dry out completely. In winter water once a week, or less if the temperature is very low. To ensure good humidity the pot can be stood over damp pebbles and the plant misted frequently.

Propagation
By seed in spring. Establish in a damp soil-based compost under a plastic cover. Or the parent plant can be divided into several smaller plants which should be repotted separately.

Repotting
This plant does not like to be moved and should only be repotted when it has outgrown its container.

PROBLEMS

If conditions are too dry the plant will be attacked by scale insect and red spider mite. Spray with a systemic insecticide and improve humidity.

The plant must never be allowed to dry out. If it does, cut back almost to soil level, immerse the pot in water for 1 hour, drain well, and keep at about 12°C/53°F until it starts to rejuvenate.

If the leaves turn yellow, the conditions may be too warm and dry. Water well, move to a cooler spot and mist frequently.

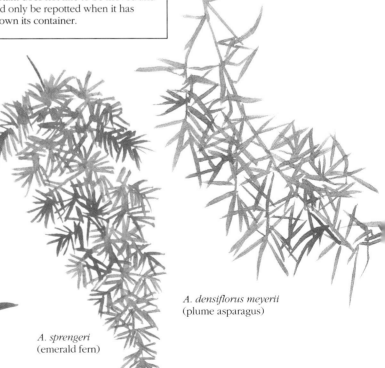

A. densiflorus meyerii
(plume asparagus)

A. sprengeri
(emerald fern)

A. falcatus

Asparagus plumosus, sometimes known as *A. setaceus,* is frequently used in floral bouquets

Asparagus plumosus (Asparagus fern)

EASY

Another from South Africa, this is a climber and can make a fresh and impressive show on a trellis, preferably made of wood, displaying its bright green, somewhat flattened, branches borne on wiry stems. As a room divider it can look extremely attractive, and is also seen climbing up around pictures and mirrors. It is frequently used in bridal bouquets.

The needle-like foliage may turn yellow and fall, either because of age or because the plant has been allowed to dry out. Red berries may form on the plant and are extremely attractive.

Care is as for other asparagus ferns outlined opposite.

Asplenium nidus (Bird's nest fern)

EASY

This exotic forest fern comes from the humid tropical areas of South East Asia and Australia, where it grows as an epiphyte in protected but constantly damp positions.

It forms a handsome rosette of lance-shaped, bright green leaves with dark central veins which will grow to almost 1m/3ft in length. These leaves are very delicate and should be cleaned carefully with a damp cloth from time to time. Do not use leaf shine.

Asplenium does well as a houseplant. It is a relatively quick grower and is at its best for 3 years, after which it should be propagated (which is difficult to do at home).

It likes a warm, humid and partly shady spot, away from draughts, but can tolerate central heating if there is sufficient humidity.

A. nidus

Asplenium nidus

CARE

Light and temperature
A semi-shady position, away from direct sunlight. The ideal temperature is 20°C/68°F all year, and no lower than 16°C/61°F in winter.

Water and feeding
Water 2–3 times a week in summer to keep the compost moist at all times. In winter water less, allowing the top of the compost almost to dry out between waterings. To ensure adequate humidity, stand the pot over damp pebbles. In spring and summer fertilize with a general houseplant solution at fortnightly intervals.

Propagation
By spore. This is difficult and best left to a professional.

Repotting
This plant does not like to be moved unnecessarily so pot on in summer only when it has become rootbound.

PROBLEMS

Prone to scale insect, which should be treated with a systemic insecticide.

Damaged or dried fronds can be cut off at the stem.

Brown spots on the leaves mean that the position is too cold and draughty. Move to a warmer, more protected spot.

Blechnum gibbum

QUITE DIFFICULT

An expansive palm-like fern with a spread of up to 1m/3ft, *Blechnum* will need a reasonable amount of space indoors. Originally from New Caledonia, it has a sturdy black trunk which grows to 1m/3ft. From this it produces a broad spread of arching pinnate fronds, some of which are fertile.

Indoors, it prefers coolish, dry conditions, though it also accommodates warm temperatures of up to 24°C/75°F as long as it has a high humidity level in the form of frequent misting and standing the pot over damp gravel. Once established, it should last for many years. Misting should keep the leaves clean.

The other common *Blechnum* is the Brazilian tree fern, *B. braziliense*.

CARE

Light and temperature
Bright but indirect light with temperatures ranging from 18–24°C/64–75°F, and no lower than 10°C/50°F in winter.

Water and feeding
Water carefully, allowing the top of the compost to dry out between waterings. As the temperature rises, increase the humidity. Use a general houseplant fertilizer at fortnightly intervals in spring and summer.

Propagation
From spores. This is difficult and best left to a professional.

Repotting
In spring, every second year, in a no. 2 peat-based compost, ensuring good drainage.

PROBLEMS

Mealy bug, scale insect and aphids can attack this plant. Remove mealy bug and scale insect with a cloth dipped in methylated spirit and spray aphids with a pyrethrum-based insecticide.

If the pinnas start to fall, the humidity must be increased. Ensure the plant stands over damp pebbles at all times and improve air circulation.

Blechnum gibbum is available in both narrow-leaved and wide-leaved varieties

Nephrolepis (Sword fern, Boston fern, fishbone fern)

EASY

This common fern, with long tapering fronds that can grow up to 1m/3ft, was a favourite in Victorian times.

It grows freely in all tropical regions of the world, from Africa to the Americas and the Far East. A good humidity is essential, and it likes warm, bright, but semi-shady conditions (as it enjoys in its native habitat) all year round.

Spray each day with tepid rain water and stand the pot over wet gravel. Never allow the compost to dry out or to become water-logged.

It is a good houseplant as it will tolerate a fairly dark position, but it does not always do well in a centrally heated room or close to a gas fire. In the right conditions *Nephrolepis* will last a long time.

Do not use insecticides or leaf shine on this plant.

PROBLEMS

Sometimes the fern will deteriorate for no apparent reason. Cut it down to just above soil level and keep warm and humid until it begins to grow again.

Dry and dropping leaves are caused by dry air. Immerse the pot in water, drain, surround the pot with damp peat, and spray daily. If it does not recover, cut it right back and treat as above.

Scale insect and mealy bug can be attracted to this plant. Remove with a cloth dipped in methylated spirit. Do not use an insecticide.

CARE

Light and temperature
Bright to semi-shady conditions, but no direct sunlight and no dry air. In summer temperatures should be 18–24°C/64–75°F and in winter 13–16°C/55–61°F.

Water and feeding
Water 2–3 times a week with room temperature water in spring and summer, and feed each week with a weak liquid fertilizer. For the rest of the year water a little less, but never allow the compost to dry out.

Propagation
From plantlets that form on runners coming out of the crown of the plant. Pot these in a peaty mixture and keep at a constant temperature of 20°C/68°F until established.

Repotting
Repot in a peat-based mixture in spring as it becomes rootbound. The plant can be divided into smaller sections at the same time.

N. cordata

'Teddy Junior'

Nephrolepis exaltata bostoniensis (the Boston fern) was, surprisingly enough, discovered in that city in 1894 and will tolerate air-conditioning

Pellaea rotundifolia (Button fern, cliff brake)

QUITE EASY

Although a fern, this native of the temperate forests of New Zealand produces a profusion of thin black stems from which grow small, arched fronds of dark green leathery leaflets. The fronds reach 20cm/8in in length and will trail over the pot, making the plant ideal for a hanging basket.

Unusually, *Pellaea* prefers fairly dry conditions. The compost must never be allowed to become waterlogged or the plant will die. It does not appreciate misting either.

If conditions are right the plant will not have a rest period and should continue to grow all year round.

CARE

Light and temperature
Fairly bright but indirect light with constant temperatures, preferably not above 21°C/71°F. Increase humidity as the temperature rises. In winter it will tolerate as low as 6°C/43°F.

Water and feeding
Keep the compost moist, but never soggy, taking care not to let the plant dry out completely. Feed with a liquid solution of general houseplant fertilizer once a week during summer.

Propagation
Divide the rhizome into 2 or 3 sections, each with roots and some growth, and establish in a mixture of loam, peat and sand.

Repotting
Pot on as needed in a shallow pot, ensuring good drainage.

PROBLEMS

Never allow the compost to get soggy or the plant will die.

Susceptible to scale insect, mealy bug and aphids. Remove scale insect and mealy bug with a cloth dipped in methylated spirit. Spray aphids with a pyrethrum-based insecticide.

Pellaea rotundifolia bears little resemblance to the commonly perceived fern

Platycerium (Staghorn fern, elkhorn fern)

EASY

This exotic fern comes from the tropical areas of Australia and Papua New Guinea, where it grows in rainforests as an epiphyte, though it does adapt quite well to indoor conditions.

As a houseplant it likes to be attached to wood, as it often is in its native habitat. It does well surrounded by peat and moss and hung from a wall or pillar and thrives well in a basket, its main fronds – up to 1m/3ft long – arching over the pot and dividing into several antler-like shapes. These fronds produce spores on their undersides, and gradually turn brown and papery before being replaced by new ones. At the back are sterile leaves which grow upright and act as a support for the plant.

Platycerium will tolerate central heating as long as it has plenty of humidity. Spray with rain water daily and this should also keep the fronds clean. Do not use leaf shine.

It should last for many years.

Platycerium alcicorne

CARE

Light and temperature
Bright light or weak direct light. The ideal temperature is 21°C/71°F all year, with plenty of humidity, and no lower than 13°C/55°F in winter.

Water and feeding
In spring and summer submerge the pot in water for 15 minutes to make the compost moist. Allow the soil to dry out between waterings. In winter, when the plant is dormant, submerge for only 5 minutes. Add a weak solution to the water 2 or 3 times during spring and summer to encourage growth.

Propagation
From spores, which is difficult and best left to a professional, or from offsets with roots removed from the base and planted in a damp compost. Cover with plastic until established.

Repotting
Not necessary.

PROBLEMS

If conditions are too dry the plant will look limp. Submerge the pot in water. Spray and water more often.

If the leaves rot, conditions are too wet and cold. Water less and move to a warmer position.

If the plant is attacked by scale insect, remove with a cloth dipped in methylated spirit.

Pteris (Ribbon fern)

QUITE EASY

One of the largest groups of fern available as a houseplant – there are more than 150 varieties – *Pteris* has adapted well to the dry atmosphere of most homes. As long as it is never allowed to dry out, this native of the temperate and subtropical areas of Australia and New Zealand should thrive, growing to 1m/3ft tall.

There are several varieties readily available, most having compact fronds with elegant ribbon-shaped leaves that may carry a cream stripe. Some species have 2 types of frond – short sterile ones which grow close to the rhizome and long fertile ones which produce spores. It is natural for the fronds to die – cut back and new ones will form. Do not use leaf shine.

It should be a long-lasting houseplant.

PROBLEMS

If the fronds turn brown the plant is too dry. Cut off the damaged fronds, submerge the pot in water then drain well. Spray daily.

If the plant has too much light the fronds will shrivel. Move to a shadier position.

It is susceptible to aphids. Spray with a pyrethrum-based insecticide.

Mealy bug and scale insect should be removed with a cloth dipped in methylated spirit.

CARE

Light and temperature
Bright but indirect light. Average room temperatures of up to 22°C/74°F will suit this plant, and not below 13°C/55°F in winter.

Water and feeding
Water plentifully in summer but ensure good drainage as the compost should never be allowed to become soggy. In winter let the soil almost dry out between waterings. Mist daily to provide humidity and place the pot over damp gravel. Feed every week in spring and summer with a general houseplant liquid fertilizer.

Propagation
Best done by spores collected from the plant in autumn and sown in early March, on a peat and sand compost in a propagator at 21°C/71°F.

Repotting
As needed, when the root system has filled the pot, using a mixture of loam, peat and sand.

Pteris cretica 'Parkeri'

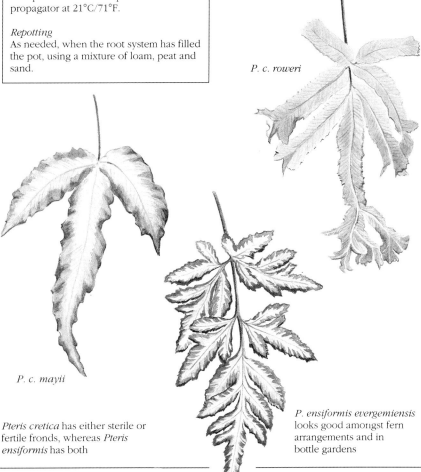

P. c. roweri

P. c. mayii

P. ensiformis evergemiensis looks good amongst fern arrangements and in bottle gardens

Pteris cretica has either sterile or fertile fronds, whereas *Pteris ensiformis* has both

Flowering Plants

Nursery men the world over are constantly seeking to improve the quality of our flowering plants: producing bigger blooms, lasting for longer periods, with new colours and greater readiness to flower.

None the less we have a wealth of beautiful and fragrant flowering plants to choose from throughout every season of the year. There are plants with richly fragrant flowers such as *Gardenia* and *Stephanotis*. There are those that are easy to grow like *Chrysanthemum* or *Clivia*, which has dramatic orange flower heads. And there are the challenging plants, such as *Columnea* or *Medinilla* – growing these successfully can be enormously rewarding.

The overriding factor for that success is the correct amount of light. After all, the flowering plants we propagate and you purchase have been adapted from ones that grow in the wild in the subtropical and tropical regions of the world. In this book, I have described these conditions so that cultivation at home can emulate them as closely as possible.

Achimenes (Hot water plant, nut orchid)

QUITE EASY

Achimenes, a member of the gesneriad family, has been popular for some 100 years

There are many folk myths associated with *Achimenes*, a plant early settlers in the United States took on their travels. Originally from Guatemala, it grows in high humidity in semi-shaded conditions.

A weak-stemmed plant, it bears masses of white, pink, blue, purple or yellow flowers throughout summer. Because its stems are weak, it is ideal for a hanging basket, where the flowers can trail downwards. It has hairy heart-shaped, jagged-edged leaves and grows up to 30cm/1ft high. After 2 or 3 years discard the plant.

There are several varieties. *Achimenes erecta* is a trailer, bearing bright red flowers. *Achimenes longiflora* has purple flowers, and there is a white variety as well. The tallest species is *Achimenes grandiflora*, which can grow to 60cm/2ft, but this is hard to find. More easily available are the *Achimenes* hybrids, which include 'Master Ingram', 'Rose Little Beauty' and 'Pink Beauty' (or 'Charm'), 'Purple King' and 'Paul Arnold'. These hybrids have been popular since the 1840s. Their flowering season is from early summer through to autumn. Never place *Achimenes* in direct sun.

CARE

Light and temperature
Bright light away from direct summer sun. Warm humid conditions with an average temperature of 13°C/55°F throughout the growing season.

Water and feeding
Never let this plant dry out, even for a single day. Spray occasionally. Feed once a fortnight with a weak liquid fertilizer during the flowering season. After blooms have finished, allow the plant to rest. Stimulate growth the following spring by watering with tepid water or else remove the rhizomes from the soil in autumn, and allow to dry off throughout the winter.

Propagation
Divide the peculiarly scaly rhizomes in early spring and plant up to 6 together in a pot about 15cm/6in across, or take cuttings in late spring in seed-raising compost and place in a propagator at a temperature of 21°C/70°F.

Repotting
The rhizomes need repotting in early spring, with the top 2.5cm/1in of soil being replaced with rich humus compost. It is easy to divide rhizomes when repotting.

PROBLEMS

Cobwebs forming on the underside of leaves indicate red spider mite. Spray with a systemic insecticide and do not allow the plant to dry out.

Leaves may become discoloured – spray less often.

If flowers do not form increase humidity and place in a lighter position, but avoiding direct sunlight.

Aphelandra squarrosa (Zebra plant, saffron spike)

DIFFICULT

There are many species of this plant, but only 2 have been hybridized as houseplants. By far the most commonly found is *Aphelandra squarrosa*, known as the zebra plant because of its distinctive leaf markings. Originally from tropical South America, this plant is greedy when it comes to humidity. Try to site it in a spot where it can stand on a tray of pebbles.

In domestic circumstances *Aphelandra* will be difficult to keep going for more than a year – leaves will fall from the base upwards and it usually becomes leggy. The stems are almost black, in stark contrast to the handsome yellow bract which appears for a month or more in autumn.

Aphelandra squarrosa 'Dania' has a striking golden bract, from which stem insignificant white flowers (though breeding by nursery men has improved this variety), and *Aphelandra squarrosa* 'Louisae' has bracts with deep orange tops. Both form reasonably bushy plants of up to 45cm/½in high and wide.

CARE

Light and temperature
Aphelandra likes bright light but no direct sun. The leaves burn easily. In summer keep at 18–27°C/64–80°F. After flowering has taken place in autumn, temperatures can drop to 12°C/55°F. Cold air will cause it to drop its leaves, as will too much sun and any hint of draughts.

Water and feeding
Always use soft warm water and never let the compost dry out. – waterlogging is fatal. Spray the leaves each day with warm water and cut off all faded bracts above a good pair of leaves. From early spring to early autumn feed on a weekly basis, and twice a week when the plant is in flower.

Propagation
In early spring take stem cuttings from leaf axils, preferably with 2 pairs of leaves, and pot up using a rooting hormone. A heated propagator must be used, and once new leaves signal the cutting has taken, pot on into a 15cm/6in container. Acclimatize the young plant carefully.

Repotting
If you have a sufficiently good specimen, repot it in spring in good compost.

PROBLEMS

Major leaf loss and brown leaf tips can be caused by dryness at the roots, even for a very short time. Other possible causes are too much sun, draughts or cold air and lack of humidity.

Cobwebs may form on the underside of leaves, indicating red spider mites caused by dryness. Use a systemic insecticide.

White woolly patches in the axils of leaves are caused by mealy bug. Spray with diluted malathion.

Aphelandra squarrosa 'Dania' has most dramatic creamy veining on its leaves

Ardisia crenata (Coral berry, spice berry)

EASY

This small and erect shrub, which grows up to 1m/3ft high, bears shiny red berries at Christmas time.

Its original habitat is the subtropical areas of Japan, where it reaches double the height it can attain as an indoor plant. It has waxy deep green leathery leaves, with tiny white or pale pink flowers that are really rather insignificant. The berries which follow are by far the most attractive feature of the plant and will last until the onset of flowering the following season. They form on almost horizontal stalks at the lower end of the plant foliage.

Ardisia will last for 3–4 years – and indeed go on for more, though it easily loses its vigour. Prune back each spring before flowering.

CARE

Light and temperature
Bright light, and some direct sun each day. Keep cool in winter and always away from draughts. It needs a minimum 9°C/45°F in winter. Never let the compost dry out and prune in spring.

Water and feeding
Always keep the compost moist, watering less often in winter than in summer. Spray often and feed each fortnight. Stand over damp pebbles if possible.

Propagation
Through stem cuttings taken in spring or summer, or seeds sown in early spring. Neither method is easy.

Repotting
When potbound, move on to a pot one size larger.

PROBLEMS

If there are few berries, use a brush to pollinate the flowers the following season.

If the plant is reluctant to flower, ensure it has high humidity during spring when the buds are forming.

Leaves become mottled with webs on the underside, indicating red spider mite. Spray with insecticide and raise humidity.

If white woolly patches appear on and in axils of leaves the plant has been infested with mealy bug. Remove with a swab dipped in methylated spirit.

If the flowers drop before the fruit is set the plant is too cold. Move to a warmer position.

Ardisia crenata should never be positioned in a draughty place

Azalea indica (Indian azalea)

QUITE DIFFICULT

Azaleas bring a sunburst of colour into the house, from scarlet to apricot to white. A member of the *Rhododendron* family and originating from China and Thailand, they are dwarf shrubs that can grow up to 45cm/1.5ft in height.

Azalea indica, or the Indian azalea, is by far the most popular. It has rich green leaves of up to 4cm/1.5in long with hairy undersides and the flowers are open and bell-shaped. It is forced into flower for winter colour but will suffer thereafter, and should not be neglected if the plant is to last until the following season.

Azaleas are usually bought when in flower. Pick one with a mass of buds, rather than blooms, so you can enjoy the spectacular show of flowers, either single or double, on top of the little flat bush. It should be watered by the immersion method (see page 232) perhaps every day when in flower.

After flowering, keep watering and place it outside during the summer. This variety is not frost-hardy, so the plant must be brought into the house when summer is over.

Azalea indica

'Osta' 'Indica' 'Inga'

CARE

Light and temperature
A pot-grown azalea loves cool temperatures. It likes good light but not direct sunshine, so a north-facing window is ideal.

Water and feeding
Keep the compost wet but not soggy at all times, using rain water. Remember azaleas hate lime. An occasional spray with rain water helps to prolong the life of the blooms. Pick off faded flowers promptly.
  If you feed the plant each fortnight it should flower again the next autumn. In spring, after the danger of frost has passed, take the pot outside and place it in a light but cool place. Keep the compost wet all season before bringing it indoors in autumn.

Propagation
Cuttings of healthy young shoots around 7cm/3in can be taken in summer and rooted in a heated propagator in the middle of summer at temperatures of 21–24°C/ 70–75°F. Use only lime-free compost and keep moist with rain water.

Repotting
After the first season and when the plant has outgrown the pot, repot in spring, always using lime-free compost and keep in the garden throughout summer.

PROBLEMS

Shrivelled or yellowing leaves, or a short flowering period are the most common complaints. Always water azaleas thoroughly, if possible soaking the entire pot each week at least. Water with soft water and always use lime-free compost.

Lime in the water causes yellowing leaves. This indicates chlorosis, caused by a lack of iron if grown in lime soil. Treat with multi-tonic and pick off the affected leaves.

Too much sun will cause the flowers to wither and brown and then drop off, as will too little humidity and too much hot dry air. Keep azaleas well away from radiators.

Begonia elatior

EASY

There are around 900 different species of *Begonia*, which is named after the Frenchman Michel Begon (1638–1710), who was a patron of botanical science.

Some species are grown for their leaf colour; others, including *Begonia elatior*, for their flowers. Two English nursery men – Veitch in the 1880s and Clibrans in the 1900s – developed *B. elatior*, which is a native of Brazil, and Dutch specialists began marketing it just after World War II.

The plant is covered by a mass of single or double flowers in cheerful colours. It can be bought in flower at any time of year and indoors will last for about 3 months.

The German *Begonia elatior* 'Reiger' strain is among the most reliable varieties, with a long-lasting flowering period, and *Begonia elatior* 'Reigers Schwabenland' is particularly recommended.

Pinching out the growing tips when the plant is young will keep it bushy. It is normally discarded after flowering, though it is possible to keep it going through 2 or 3 flowerings.

Begonia tuberosa

Begonia elatior
'Reiger'

The flower head of
Begonia elatior

Begonia elatior

Begonia elatior in its varied colours

B. tuber-hybrida 'Harlequin'

CARE

Light and temperature
Begonia prefers a light position, but not direct sunlight, which will scorch the leaves and flowers. Temperatures above 20°C/70°F are best avoided.

Water and feeding
When the plant is in flower, water often, but do not allow the soil to become soggy. Spray the foliage and flowers to keep moist air around the plant, but do not do this when the plant is in direct sunlight. Feeding is not strictly necessary, as the plant is usually discarded after flowering.

Propagation
Some varieties, like the double orange 'Charisma', can be raised from seed. Otherwise, new shoots can be used as cuttings.

Repotting
If raising from seed, pot on the seedlings only once after they reach flowering size.

PROBLEMS

Begonia is prone to powdery mildew. Cut off the diseased leaves and spray with a systemic fungicide. Improving ventilation and cutting back on watering often helps.

Botrytis causes brown, grey and mouldy patches and can be avoided by the same treatments as for powdery mildew.

Aphids and red spider mites need to be sprayed with appropriate insecticides.

Too little light and too little or too much water can cause yellowing of the leaves. If stems become long and leggy, there is inadequate light. Leaves will curl up if there is too much heat and they will rot and droop if the plant is overwatered.

The leaves will need to be sprayed with water if they develop brown tips.

If the plant collapses, the causes are most often stem rot disease (caused by overwatering), swollen bumps on the tubers (known as root knot), eelworm or vine weevil, which causes tunnels in the tuberous stems.

Beloperone guttata (Shrimp plant)

EASY

Beloperone guttata is sometimes listed as *Justicia brandegeana*

CARE

Light and temperature
The stems of the shrimp plant become quite woody and if there is too much heat they will become softened and the plant will grow straggly. Temperatures of 20°C/71°F in summer and 18°C/64°F in winter will suit this plant. To produce colourful bracts it will need direct sunlight. This should be for relatively short periods in summer on a windowsill.

Water and feeding
Keep moist but not wet from spring to autumn, but drier in the winter months. Feed each fortnight during summer with a weak solution of houseplant fertilizer.

Propagation
In spring cut back the stems to 10cm/3in above the soil and repot at the same time. Tips of shoots can be rooted in a propagator at 18°C/64°F.

Repotting
In spring, prune back plants to around half their size and repot in good compost.

This small oval-leafed plant can survive for many years and grows up to 90cm/3ft square. Keep pruning out the stem tips to make the plant bushier and disregard those who tell you it is an annual.

The reddy-orange flower bracts are like overlapping Tuscan roof tiles and support a white flower which emerges at the end. The bracts appear almost all year round but the white flowers are insignificant and short-lived.

Beloperone guttata's native habitat is the tropical areas of Mexico, where it grows under tall trees. As an indoor plant it is very adaptable and cuttings can be rooted easily. There is a yellow form called 'Yellow Queen', which may be found on supermarket shelves from time to time.

Clever use can be made of this plant in hanging baskets.

PROBLEMS

The plant will lose leaves if it becomes rootbound. Repot if necessary.

If leaves turn yellow, the plant has been overwatered. Allow the compost to dry out thoroughly before watering again.

Spray the plant with insecticide if it is attacked by aphids during hot weather; this is all too common.

If bracts do not develop, prune especially hard at the onset of the dormant period, and in early spring place the plant on an extremely sunny windowsill.

Bougainvillea glabra (Paper flower)

'White Dania'

'Amethyst'

'Afterglow'

DIFFICULT

This is a glorious tropical climber, with dazzling purplish-pink bracts in groups of three which develop in spring and summer and last a long time. It is not an easy houseplant to grow or to make bloom again the next season. The stems are woody with spines and the leaves are narrow and smooth. In its native habitat of Brazil, it will grow to 9m/30ft but reaches considerably less when kept in a pot.

There are many different species, but I would say the most successful is *Bougainvillea glabra* 'Alexandra'. *Bougainvillea spectabilis* is altogether larger with stout spines. Its bracts measure up to 5cm/2in square and the plant has a spreading habit. Commonly found varieties include the American 'Crimson Lake' or 'Scarlett O'Hara' and the European 'Amethyst' and 'White Dania'.

This plant needs to be pruned in autumn and kept cool throughout the winter. Many bougainvilleas are available trained on hoops but they can also be found as standards or bushes.

Bougainvillea glabra 'Alexandra'

CARE

Light and temperature
Keep the plant warm in summer; it will appreciate a spell outdoors baking in the sun. Maintain a minimum winter temperature of 7°C/45°F.

Water and feeding
When spring arrives, increase watering from once a fortnight to 2–3 times a week and feed the plant every 2 weeks with a weak solution of liquid fertilizer. It will need doses of potassium fertilizer each spring. Spray with tepid water on warm days and keep the compost moist in spring and summer, but almost dry in winter.

Propagation
In spring. Use 8–10cm/3–4in cuttings dipped in hormone rooting powder. Place in a propagator at a constant temperature of 21–24°C/70–75°F with high humidity. Many of the leaves may drop. This is, however, a difficult plant to root and propagation is best left to professionals.

Repotting
Repot in spring, and only when the existing pot has been outgrown. Use standard compost to which has been added some woodash. Sphagnum peat moss also helps.

PROBLEMS

Bad ventilation and a humidity level that is too high will cause mealy bugs. Spray with an insecticide.

Cobwebs underneath the leaves are caused by red spider mite due to the plant becoming dry. Use a systemic insecticide.

Yellowing of leaves is caused by the plant being too wet. Always ensure the compost has very good drainage.

Bouvardia (Sweet bouvardia, scarlet trompetilla)

DIFFICULT

This is a gloriously scented plant with trusses of pink or white 4-lobed flowers which come out from summer through to midwinter. Originally from Mexico, it is similar to *Ixora* as both of these species belong to the madder family.

Bouvardia lasts for only a couple of years, even when it has had the most expert and loving attention. It is valued for the time of year it blooms and for its scent as much as anything else.

Prune it vigorously in early spring and keep it on the dry side through a good period of rest during the early summer months.

CARE

Light and temperature
Bright light, but keep shaded from direct summer sun. Minimum temperatures of 10°C/50°F in autumn help to set flower buds. Room temperature in summer.

Water and feeding
Water freely while the plant is flowering and feed each fortnight. After flowering, allow compost to dry out between waterings.

Propagation
Through stem cuttings taken in spring.

Repotting
Should be repotted each spring in a mixture of general purpose soil, perlite and peat.

B. longifolia has the most delightful scented white flowers

B. ternifolia can bear its scarlet blossoms for much of the year

Bouvardia 'Bridesmaid'

PROBLEMS

Webs on the underside of leaves indicate red spider mite. Spray with a systemic insecticide and raise humidity.

If the plant droops it is too cold or too dry.

If the leaves dry out move the plant to a cooler spot.

Browallia (Bush violet, amethyst flower, sapphire flower)

EASY

With proper care and attention, this dainty, simple plant can bloom for weeks. In fact it is often bought for its long flowering period and then thrown out. *Browallia speciosa* flowers naturally during the second half of the year, depending on the time of sowing, and looks particularly effective when massed with others as a group.

From tropical Colombia, the plant grows up to 50cm/20in in height and has dark green leaves with blue, lavender and white flowers. Some plants need stakes to support the stems. The more the plant is pinched out in its early growing days the better. You should pick off the dead flowers regularly and discard the plant when the flowering season is over.

The variety 'Major' produces large blue flowers, while 'Alba' has white blooms. The only other *Browallia* found as an indoor plant is *Browallia viscosa*, which is smaller than the bush violet and has white-throated flowers that are more subtle.

The bush violet, being a member of the deadly nightshade family, and therefore poisonous, should be kept well out of the reach of children and animals.

Browallia speciosa can look extremely effective in a hanging basket

CARE

Light and temperature
Browallia likes a bright position, but not direct sunlight. Give it 4 good hours of strong light a day. It needs to be in temperatures of around 20°C/68°F in summer (temperatures much over this will reduce the life of the flowers), and cooler in winter.

Water and feeding
In summer water often, always keeping the soil moist, and feed each week. In winter water sparingly, otherwise the roots may rot. Humidity is important so if possible place on a tray of wet pebbles.

Propagation
This plant grows easily from seed; sow in early spring. The seeds will sprout within 14 days. Cover with a dusting of compost and place in a propagator at 18°C/64°F. After the seedlings have germinated, prick off into 7.5cm/3in pots. They will begin to flower 6 months later.

Repotting
Not necessary as most people regard this plant as an annual.

PROBLEMS

When the air is dry, greenfly and whitefly can sometimes be a nuisance. Spray with insecticide.

If the plant becomes leggy, pinch out the growth tips to encourage bushiness.

Brunfelsia (Yesterday, today and tomorrow or morning, noon and night)

QUITE EASY

The common name of this sweet-smelling plant refers to its changing colours: the flowers move from purple through pale violet to white in fast succession.

It is an extremely slow growing but very attractive plant, with glossy green leaves and pretty flowers about 5cm/2in across. In its native habitat of Brazil, where it is found in tropical conditions under semi-shaded canopy, it will grow to 2m/8ft tall, but as an indoor plant it rarely reaches above 60cm/2ft. It can flower almost all year round, and will be particularly encouraged if placed in a sheltered spot on a sunny patio during the summer months.

CARE

Light and temperature
Keep out of direct sun when growing and in flower. During spring and summer keep temperature between 18–24°C/64–75°F. This plant flush flowers so to encourage a second flowering it is important to drop the temperature to 13°C/55°F. After this second flush and with winter approaching, reduce temperatures further to 7°C/45°F to harden off plant.

Water and feeding
Water thoroughly in spring and summer. Stand the pot on a saucer of pebbles almost covered with water since the plant enjoys high humidity. In winter, remove from pebbles and allow to dry out between waterings. During spring and summer feed at monthly intervals with general houseplant fertilizer.

Propagation
Take tip cuttings and place in cutting compost in a propagator at a temperature between 18–21°C/64–70°F.

Repotting
In autumn, when flowering has finished, in no. 2 loam-based compost.

PROBLEMS

Webs on underside of leaves indicate red spider mite. Use systemic insecticide or diluted malathion and raise humidity.

Grey mould may occur in winter if plant is too cold and too wet.

Brunfelsia pauciflora calycina can be found with white or yellow flowers as well as the more common purple variety

Calceolaria herbeohybrida (Pocketbook plant)

EASY

CARE

Light and temperature
Calceolaria likes bright light, but should be protected from the midday sun in a cool and airy position, perhaps a north window. Ideal temperatures are 10–13°C/50–55°F.

Water and feeding
Water well, and spray occasionally, but do not allow the compost to become too wet. Feed weekly during flowering.

Propagation
Generally this is best tackled by professionals.

Repotting
Not necessary as the plant is an annual.

PROBLEMS

Flowers may turn brown if the plant is too hot and dry. Move to a cooler location.

Prone to greenfly. Spray with a systemic insecticide.

This cheerful plant, with unusual pouch-shaped flowers, in blotchy yellow, orange, red or white, rising above large hairy leaves, is bought in flower and has a relatively short life as an indoor plant. None the less it produces an eye-catching splash of colour in the early months of the year. Keep the temperature on the cool side to prolong the flowering season.

The name of the plant derives from the Latin word *calceolus*, meaning small shoe. Originally *Calceolaria* was found on the lower slopes of the Andes mountains of Chile and it reaches about 45cm/18in high. It is best regarded as an annual.

Calceolaria integrifolia (Chilean pouch or slipper flower) looks similar but is grown as an annual, for flowering tubs on patios or in public parks.

Campanula isophylla (Italian bellflower, star of Bethlehem, falling stars)

EASY

Nearly all campanulas are hardy garden plants, but only a few of the 35 genera are suitable as houseplants. By far the most reliable and dazzling of these is *Campanula isophylla*. With its pale green leaves setting off star-shaped blue or white flowers, it is best displayed from a suspended pot or hanging basket. Although blue is the most common colour, a white variety, *Campanula isophylla* 'alba', and a mauve variety, *Campanula isophylla* 'Mayii' (which is difficult to grow), are more readily available these days.

This pretty subtropical plant is a native of Italy and grows to a height of 22cm/9in with a spread of 45cm/18in. It should flower happily throughout the summer. Pinch off flower heads that have faded, and give the bush a sharp trim as the flowering season ends. The plant should be replaced after a couple of years.

C. isophylla 'alba'

C. isophylla

CARE

Light and temperature
Campanula likes bright positions with as much light as possible, but in summer protect it from the hot noon sun. It likes average warmth. Good periods of rest in winter will help the plant to be a successful flowerer the following season. In winter it will tolerate below-freezing temperatures. Adequate ventilation is essential.

Water and feeding
In the flowering season keep the plant moist at all times. Apply liquid fertilizer every fortnight to prolong the blooms. In late winter, cut the plant right back to within 3cm/1in of the soil, leaving 1 pair of leaves. Keep on the dry side, watering only occasionally. Vigorous new growth will appear in spring. Then water the plant regularly. Do not use leaf shine.

Propagation
Start cuttings off in spring from prunings made when cutting the plant back. Tips need to be 10cm/4in long and inserted into a peat and sand compost and placed in a propagating frame with a constant temperature of 18°C/64°F.

Repotting
Repot once in spring, after the first season, using a rich humus potting soil.

PROBLEMS

If leaves turn yellow and fall, red spider mites could be infesting the plant. Spray with a systemic insecticide.

Conditions that are too wet and cold cause flowers to rot and fall before opening. Stand in a warmer atmosphere and allow to dry out before watering again.

Waterlogging can cause the leaves and stems to rot. Allow the plant to dry out.

Should mould appear, apply a fungicide to kill the fungus. Make sure the compost is not left saturated in humid conditions.

C. carpatica 'Karl Foster'

C. carpatica 'Karl Foster' white

C. poscharskyana white

C. poscharskyana blue

Canna hybrida (Canna lily, Indian shot)

EASY

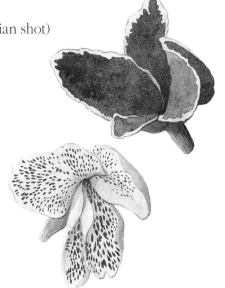

An indoor bulb which cannot tolerate frost, the canna lily will appreciate a sunny patio after flowering but should never be left outside in winter.

It is a wonderfully colourful plant with large clusters of flowers, on a 60–90cm/2–3ft stalk, which last for 3 weeks or so.

Its native habitat is mostly Brazil, where it grows in tropical conditions in the rainforests.

Dutch and Danish growers have bred a wide variety of colours – reds, pinks, yellows and white. The flowers can be up to 12cm/5in across and many are striped or spotted, though the pure white ones are the most dramatic against the green, dark green or purple leaves. This lily is summer-blooming and should be left in its pot until the foliage has completely died down. The compost should be kept almost dry until growth begins again the next spring.

The canna lily loses its vigour after 4 or 5 years and should be replaced.

Canna indica

CARE

Light and temperature
During the growing period give plenty of light and average room temperatures. Protect from scorching midday sun, particularly when flowering, to make the flowers last longer. Winter rest in a box of peat is recommended.

Water and feeding
Water frequently to keep the soil moist during the flowering season. Ensure good drainage. Feed with a weak solution of liquid fertilizer to encourage growth of the flower stalk. After flowering allow the plant to die down with minimal watering prior to a period of dormancy.

Propagation
Best left to a professional.

Repotting
This bulb likes a rich houseplant compost when repotted easily each spring after the dormant period. Begin watering right away.

PROBLEMS

Mealy bugs can infest this plant. Treat individually and raise the humidity around the plant.

If flowers fail to form, try increasing the dormancy period and ensure the bulb is kept in really cool, though frost-free, conditions for at least 3 months. Thereafter apply fertilizer when watering.

Capsicum annuum (Ornamental chilli pepper, Christmas pepper)

EASY

CARE

Light and temperature
The plant needs to be in a sunny and airy position, but not too hot. Some direct sun is needed. In dim light, it will immediately shed its fruit. It prefers moderate temperatures.

Water and feeding
Keep damp, but not wet, and feed weekly during the growing period with weak solutions of liquid fertilizer.

Propagation
Ornamental chilli peppers can be grown from seed planted in a propagator in winter. If the seedlings are placed outside on a warm patio during summer they will bear more fruit than those continuously indoors.

Repotting
These plants are annuals.

Capsicum fruits profusely and the peppers last up to 3 months

Capsicum annuum is usually available in autumn, when its bright red fruits add festive cheer to windowsills and tables in the period leading up to Christmas.

The plant should be purchased in September, when the starlike white flowers are in bud. From these develop green peppers which ripen into purple, crimson and orangy-yellow edible fruits. It must not be confused with the poisonous *Solanum pseudocapsicum*. The plant grows to a height of 45cm/18in, and lasts only 1 season.

The ornamental pepper is native to Central South America, where it grows as a small tropical shrub.

PROBLEMS

Aphids and spider mites can infest the plant if it is put in a place which is too warm and dry. Move to a cooler position and spray with insecticide.

If the peppers fall the chances are the compost has been allowed to dry out. Increase watering. If this appears not to be the cause, increase humidity by placing the pot over a saucer of damp gravel.

Celosia cristata (Cockscomb)

EASY

This is a weird looking plant, its bright crimson, orange or yellow flowers having a velvet-like texture. The flowers are best described as cockscombs and have a greasy feel to them.

Celosia cristata grows to 45cm/18in and is quite distinct from the other main type, *Celosia plumosa* (the plume flower), which bears red or yellow feathery plumes in summer and grows to about 30cm/12in. Both originate from the cooler areas of tropical Asia, where they grow in semi-shaded areas, often clinging to rocks in the East Indies.

Although they can be raised from seed, nursery-bought plants are generally more successful. They are best regarded as annuals.

C. plumosa will have blooms for 2 months or more

Celosia cristata

CARE

Light and temperature
This plant is not fond of heat so a cool temperature of 13–15°C/55–60°F suits it best. In higher temperatures it tends to fade quickly. However it likes good light and can even have a little direct sunlight each day.

Water and feeding
Keep the compost moist at all times, but do not overwater as the plant may rot or wilt and never recover. Feed with a general indoor fertilizer each fortnight.

Propagation
Seeds can be sewn in spring at 15–18°C/60–64°F. Prick out the seedlings as soon as they are large enough to handle and pot on using a soil- or peat-based compost.

Repotting
Not necessary, as the plant is an annual. Discard after flowering.

PROBLEMS

Whitefly can be a nuisance. When infested, spray with insecticide.

Chrysanthemum

EASY

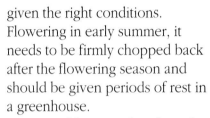

Potted chrysanthemums are now available all year round in almost every colour except blue. The Danes and the Dutch are developing many new and better varieties, with single or double flowers, in dwarf sizes, bushes or standards.

Chrysanthemum morifolium, or the florists' chrysanthemum, has been cultivated for over 3000 years in China and Japan, where it grows to 1m/3¼ft high and flowers naturally after the summer. The variety sold in stores today is *Chrysanthemum indicum*, which has been adapted to last longer in flower and is raised with the use of both chemicals and light restriction (the first curtailing growth; the second forcing flowering to a specific date). This plant is sold at a height of 24–30cm/9–12in and flowers throughout the year. It should be bought with coloured buds since green buds may fail to open.

Chrysanthemum frutescens (the white marguerite, or the Boston or Paris daisy) is altogether different and grows up to 90cm/ 36in high and 60cm/24in wide. It is also known as *Argyranthemum frutescens chrysaster*. The bush is covered by masses of small yellow or white daisy-shaped flowers which bloom for weeks on end. It may last for 3–4 years,

given the right conditions. Flowering in early summer, it needs to be firmly chopped back after the flowering season and should be given periods of rest in a greenhouse.

C. morifolium can be planted in the garden when flowering is over; this is a better long-term solution than trying to make these forced specimens last a second flowering period.

The flowering season lasts 6–8 weeks if sited in a bright, cool room; overheated rooms cause the plant to have a short life.

CARE

Light and temperature
Chrysanthemums need to be kept cool, around 13–16°C/55–60°F and in a bright position. Pot chrysanthemums must not be subjected to direct midday sun.

Water and feeding
In summer the plant needs to be kept thoroughly moist, which may mean watering it frequently. In winter, keep the compost just moist. Feed with fertilizer each fortnight while the plant is in flower.

Propagation
C. frutescens and *C. morifolium* can be raised from seed or cuttings in spring and potted into large containers of soil-based compost as necessary. They can then be brought indoors in the autumn, which is the natural flowering time for garden chrysanthemums. Pot-grown dwarf chrysanthemums can be pruned and planted outside in the garden after flowering, or be treated as annuals and discarded. If planted outdoors, they revert to the natural flowering season in autumn and grow taller as the effect of the dwarf hormones given to them by nursery men wears off.

Repotting
In spring, when necessary, using good potting compost.

PROBLEMS

Aphids and spider mites can infest the plants if they are too warm. Move to a cooler spot and spray with insecticide.

Chrysanthemum frutescens

Citrus mitis (Calamondin orange)

QUITE EASY

This miniature orange tree brings threefold pleasure. Its leaves are wonderfully glossy and dark green and carry deliciously fragrant tiny white flowers, borne singly on the branch tips, and decorative edible, if bitter, fruits.

From the Philippines, *Citrus mitis* is a dwarf variety and grows up to 1.2m/4ft high. It may well be a hybrid of the lime and the kumquat. Flowers and fruits develop throughout the year, though the greatest profusion will come in summer. A spell in the garden during this time will benefit the orange tree and may avoid the need to brush-pollinate the flowers. Midday is the best time to artifically aid pollination.

A gentle shake when buying the plant will ensure you do not choose one whose leaves are falling – a sign of an unhealthy specimen. Draughts should be avoided at all times. With good plant management *Citrus mitis* can last for years.

CARE

Light and temperature
Citrus mitis likes a bright, sunny position throughout the year and a spell outdoors in summer. In winter, temperatures of 15–18°C/60–64°F will suit it well. Good ventilation without draughts is important.

Water and feeding
Always use soft water and do not let the soil dry out between spring and autumn. In the growing period, use a weak solution of fertilizer each week.

Propagation
This is difficult to do in the domestic environment, but enthusiasts can try in spring. Dip cuttings in a rooting hormone powder and plant into a rich compost in a base-heated propagator. Plants grown from orange pips are too large for indoor plants in the long run.

Repotting
Lack of new growth indicates soil exhaustion. Repot in spring into a pot one size up when the plant is very potbound.

PROBLEMS

Citrus is prone to scale insect. Remove individually with methylated spirit swabs.

Spider mites, aphids and mealy bug may attack the plant from time to time. Spray with fungicides or insecticides.

If the leaves develop patches of dark grey mould, spray with a systemic fungicide.

Yellow leaves may appear if the plant has been watered using hard water. They may also be a sign of lack of magnesium. Add a plant tonic with magnesium to remedy this.

Brown-tipped leaves indicate the plant may be suffering from draughts. Move to a better site.

Citrus mitis has loose-skinned fruits around 5cm/2in across; they make a good addition to marmalade

Clerodendrum thomsonae

EASY

(Glory bower, bleeding heart vine)

This is a vigorous climbing shrub in the tropical regions of west Africa, where it grows up to 4m/13ft on twining stems, supporting itself on other vegetation. It has attractive dark glossy leaves with startling papery white flowers that have blood-red corollas appearing throughout the summer season.

Here nursery men treat the plant with growth inhibitors and it is sold as a shrub reaching no more that 60cm/2ft high. The plant will live for 4 or 5 years as an indoor plant before becoming too straggly and losing its vigour. Even so, pruning is necessary to encourage further flowering after new growth appears and to keep the plant in check; cut back up to half the previous year's growth. *Clerodendrum* flowers on new growth and the weak stems will need to be supported.

Keep it in a cool place during winter as it cannot cope with heating units or air conditioning.

Clerodendrum thomsonae can look striking in a hanging basket but it is important to pinch out the stem tips to prevent legginess

PROBLEMS

If the air is too dry, flowers and buds can drop off. Keep the air around the plant humid by spraying.

If the plant does not flower, the humidity and temperature must be increased during the growing period.

Spray with a systemic insecticide if the plant is infested with whitefly. White woolly patches on the axils of leaves indicate mealy bug. Spray with diluted malathion.

CARE

Light and temperature
Very bright, but no direct sun. It needs warmth and humidity. Allow it to rest during winter when it loses it leaves.

Water and feeding
Clerodendrum likes warm soft water. Do not let the plant dry out and feed once a week from spring to autumn with a high-nitrogen fertilizer. Make sure there is plenty of humus in the compost at all times, and if possible stand the pot over a tray of moist pebbles.

Propagation
This plant is difficult to propagate and requires a heated propagator if the 10cm/4in cuttings taken in spring are to grow. Dip them in hormone rooting powder and allow 6–8 weeks for new growth to appear.

Repotting
Every spring, cut back and pot on in good peaty compost which has had plenty of leafmould worked into it.

Clivia miniata (Kafir lily)

EASY

From Natal in South Africa, this rhizome develops heads of between 8–10 pretty orange bell-shaped flowers from thick stalks surrounded by glossy leaves. Varieties with red, yellow or cream flowers may occasionally be found as indoor plants.

A subtropical plant originally, it grows amongst rocks and crevices in damp and shaded conditions. It reaches 45cm/1.5ft in height and will flower regularly in early spring, but only when certain rules are obeyed: it needs space, winter rest and does not like to be repotted unless it is absolutely bursting out. Remove the dead flower stalk. The plant will benefit from a spell outdoors during the summer months.

Clivia lives for many years and is a striking plant.

Clivia miniata

CARE

Light and temperature
Bright light, but no direct sun, and cool or average warmth. Keep at a temperature of 8°C/50°F through the dormant period and at room temperature in summer.

Water and feeding
Water moderately in summer but hardly at all in winter. Always ensure good drainage. As soon as the flower stalk emerges from the base of the plant, feed on a weekly basis with general liquid fertilizer until the end of summer. Mist the leaves frequently.

Propagation
In early spring separate young offshoots after flowering with a sharp knife, ensuring the young plant retains its roots. Several growing in the same pot look attractive. The offsets may take 2 or 3 years to flower.

Repotting
Do this only when essential. Established plants only require the top 8cm/3in of soil to be changed using a soil-based compost.

PROBLEMS

White woolly patches on leaves indicate mealy bug. Remove with a swab dipped in methylated spirit.

If leaves become brown and scorched, move the plant out of the sun and do not water in direct sunlight.

Flowers may fall prematurely, in which case move to a cooler position.

If no flower spike appears once the plant has reached maturity, wait a further year and allow a longer winter resting period. Ensure correct watering takes place during the growing phase.

Columnea (Goldfish plant)

DIFFICULT

Columnea gloriosa is one of the most striking of all hanging plants, with long green tendrils producing red, orange and scarlet tubular-shaped flowers which appear at various times of the year. It is, of course, ideal for a conservatory where its glorious shape can be shown off to good effect. Its natural habitat is Central America, mainly in the dense jungles of Costa Rica, and it was named after the sixteenth-century Italian botanist, Fabius Columna.

Columnea gloriosa has trailing stems with hairy leaves and grows to 90cm/36in or more, while the hybrid *Columnea stavanger* has smooth leaves on stems which grow to the same length. *Columnea banksii* is one of the most commonly available and is also one of the easiest to make do well.

But be warned – it is a fussy plant that requires constant attention, most importantly high humidity and an enforced period of rest during winter. It will do well for 3 or 4 years and should then be replaced with new plants.

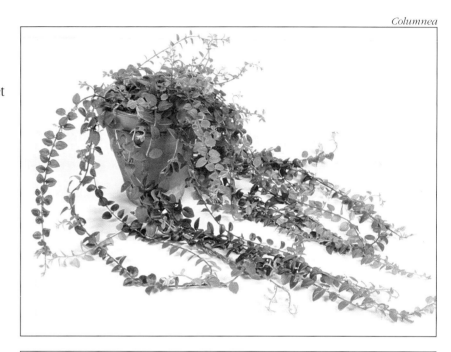

Columnea

C. banksii   C. gloriosa

CARE

Light and temperature
Bright light, but not direct sunshine. It does not like temperatures to fall below 13°C/55°F and will take up to 24°C/75°F as long as there is good humidity. The foliage will scorch if it touches the hot glass of a window.

Water and feeding
Columnea needs frequent, often daily, misting, but do not spray in direct sunlight otherwise the flowers may scorch. Avoid hard water and alkaline fertilizers. During summer, keep the soil moist but not wet, otherwise root rot or botrytis will set in. In winter keep the soil slightly damp, almost dry. Feed weekly in summer with a weak solution of liquid fertilizer. If possible, stand the plant on a bed of moist pebbles to provide a humid atmosphere.

Propagation
Use a heated propagator and take cuttings when the flowering season ends. Dip them in rooting hormone powder and plant into a rich compost of sand and loam. Make sure the cuttings are not allowed to dry out. They should take in about 3 weeks.

Repotting
Repot every 2 years after blooming into a humus-rich compost.

PROBLEMS

If the trailers become straggly, prune them by about half their length after flowering to encourage bushiness.

Draughts and central heating will cause leaves to drop. Spray the foliage daily with lime-free water.

Red spider mite can attack this plant. Treat with a systemic insecticide and then improve the humidity of the plant to prevent further attacks.

If flowers fail to appear, move the plant to a brighter spot.

Crossandra infundibuliformis

QUITE DIFFICULT

(Firecracker flower)

As the common name suggests, this is a striking plant with trumpet-shaped flame-coloured flowers in yellow, orange and red, hiding the green triangular bracts on which they form. It was brought from India in the early 1800s, but sank in popularity and was only re-introduced in the 1950s after a Swedish nursery man bred a houseplant variety, 'Mona Wallhead', which is commonly available today. The flowers are salmon-pink.

In its native habitat, *Crossandra* can grow as tall as 90cm/36in, but the indoor plants available only reach 30cm/12in high. It is a pretty, bushy plant which flowers from late spring to early autumn. It starts to flower when only a few months old. With careful plant management *Crossandra* will bloom practically throughout the year and will welcome a spell out on a sunny terrace in summer.

It needs to be sprayed often and flourishes best when it is surrounded by other plants. It will do well for up to 2 years, but should then be replaced.

CARE

Light and temperature
It likes bright light in winter and needs to be warm all year round, with temperatures no lower than 18°C/64°F. In summer place in a bright well-lit position where the plant will get some sunlight.

Water and feeding
In summer water frequently and always use water at room temperature. Do not spray either foliage or flowers. In winter, water only when the soil has dried out. Feed during the growing period.

Propagation
In early spring, top cuttings root well in a heated propagator, taking up to 6 weeks. Pot them on and pinch out the growing tips to achieve an elegantly shaped plant.

Repotting
Each spring into a pot one size larger. Good drainage is essential as overwatering is often fatal.

PROBLEMS

Red spider mite can infest the plant. Spray with insecticide.

If you notice leaves falling and the plant looking droopy, consider draughts and move the plant if necessary.

Lack of growth will be caused by not enough heat. These 'tropical' plants like warmth. Move to a better position.

If flowers do not appear, increase feeding and move to a warmer site. Pinching out leaf growth will stimulate flowering.

The stems of the Firecracker flower grow from the leaf axils; there are yellow and orange flowered varieties available too

Cyclamen persicum (Alpine violet, florist's cyclamen)

QUITE DIFFICULT

This is, deservedly, among the most popular of all flowering plants. In full bloom it is glorious in winter time, with beautiful flowers in a range of colours on long stalks above big heart-shaped leaves in variegated shades of green and silver.

Originally from the Mediterranean region, cyclamen corms grow in poor alkaline soil and in rock crevasses, and like dappled light in semi-shaded conditions. The varieties available commercially have often been forced into flower and can drop dead on you: buy only from a trusted source and never a plant that looks droopy. It likes cool conditions and a north-facing windowsill is ideal. Alpine violets, as the name suggests, can withstand slight frosts and may be planted in window boxes, where they will keep throughout the winter in temperate zones.

There are 3 main varieties, each coming in many different shades of pink, red, white and purple. Some have contrastingly coloured 'eyes'. *Cyclamen persicum* has a height and spread of 30cm/12in. The original species had a delicate scent, but this, sadly, has been bred out of modern plants. New scented varieties are currently being introduced.

The intermediate variety grows to a height and spread of 25cm/9in. It is compact and fast-growing, often bearing more than 30 flowers at a time.

The miniature varieties reach only 15cm/6in or less and bear dainty flowers in a wide range of colours. The 'Puppet' and 'Kaori' series have slightly scented flowers.

Most cyclamens are discarded after a few weeks, but with the right care and attention, they can bloom for up to 2 months in winter, and be kept going for a few years. However it is not worth much effort in trying to recover a plant that has been severely stressed by over- or underwatering.

CARE

Light and temperature
A bright but not sunny spot, airy but not too warm. Optimum winter temperatures are around 15°C/60°F: In summer, when the plant is dormant, place it outside in a semi-shaded position. Good air circulation helps.

Water and feeding
Keep the plant moist but not wet. In summer, reduce water intake. *Cyclamen* is very sensitive to too much water, which is the most common cause of its collapse. Water by standing in a bowl of water at room temperature and then allow to drain thoroughly. Never water the top of the corm where the leaves and flower stalks are clustered. Feed weekly before and during flowering. Pull out old leaves and flowers, as the old stalks rot quickly and

this rot can spread to the rest of the plant. Do not spray flowers as this may cause them to become spotted, but give the plant adequate humidity.

Propagation
Sow from seed in late summer at 18–20°C/ 64–70°F using a heated propagator. Cover the seeds with soil and pot up when germinated. Give young plants a lot of light. Most varieties will take up to 18 months to flower, but the miniature varieties take only half that length of time.

Repotting
In midsummer when the old leaves die back, repot using fresh compost – up to half of the corm should be above soil level – and stand the pot in a cool but bright position.

Cyclamen persicum

PROBLEMS

Too much hot dry air causes the leaves to yellow. Other causes may be too little water or too much sunlight.

If the plant collapses and rots, the cause is likely to be overwatering. Allow it to dry out. Never water the corm.

Shortened blooming periods can be the result of too much warm dry air and insufficient fertilizer.

Minute cyclamen mites may infect the plant, causing curled leaf edges, stunted leaves and withered buds. This pest flourishes in humid conditions and all infected leaves must be destroyed. Insecticide is of no use.

Lack of sunlight and too much heat may cause new leaves to have very long, weedy stems and will discourage new flowers.

Euphorbia milii (Christ plant, crown of thorns)

EASY

Euphorbia milii 'Selene'

Euphorbia milii 'Rosemarie'

CARE

Light and temperature
Average warmth and as much light as possible. During the flowering period it will do well in temperatures up to 18°C/64°F. Let this temperature drop by only a few degrees in winter.

Water and feeding
As a succulent, water the plant moderately, and scarcely at all in winter. Use cactus fertilizer in the water every 2 weeks while the plant is in flower.

Propagation
Take cuttings and dip them in tepid water to halt the flow of milky sap. Leave them to dry off for 24 hours and then pot in a peat and sand mixture. Keep the cuttings very much on the dry side. Once they have rooted, which takes around 6 weeks, situate in bright light. Make sure there is good drainage.

Repotting
Young plants can be repotted every 2 years. Use cactus soil. Prune or trim before new growth begins in spring.

This euphorbia, among the 2000 or more known species of the spurge family, is an old trooper. It is not fussy, and can produce cheery bracts of orange to salmon-pink and red all year round.

It comes from Madagascar, where it grows happily in granite crevasses, reaching up to 1m/40in, though as a houseplant it rarely exceeds this height. Its long thorny branches are about as thick as a little finger and are easily trained over a hoop.

Euphorbia lophogona, again from Madagascar, is an evergreen with pink flowers. The two species have been crossed to produce *Euphorbia* hybrids in a range of colours from yellow and pink through to violet.

Euphorbia milii is poisonous, particularly the juice from the woody stems.

PROBLEMS

If the leaves drop, check that there is adequate drainage, that the plant is not overwatered and that it is in a warm enough spot. The leaves grow only on new growth and will not be replaced if they fall.

The *Euphorbia* should flower for much of the year. If it fails to, move it to the sunniest spot you have.

Euphorbia pulcherrima (Poinsettia, Christmas star, Mexican flame leaf)

DIFFICULT

In its native Mexico, the tropical *Euphorbia pulcherrima* often climbs to 3m/10ft or more. It flowers when the days are shortest, hence our ability to adapt it to indoors. The Americans were instrumental in developing the plant during the 1960s, from the original which was first recorded in 1834. Today we prepare over 7 acres of poinsettias for sale into the Christmas trade.

The plant grows only to about 45cm/1½ft. The flowers, which are really coloured bracts, make a wonderful show in cream, yellow, pink or red and should last for 2–3 months. There are single-stemmed or standard forms available commercially. 'Pulcherrima' means 'the most beautiful'.

Most people treat this plant as an annual and throw it away after flowering so never buy a specimen whose leaves are falling. It is difficult, but not impossible, to make it flower again. Pinch out the growing tips to help the plant become bushy.

To achieve flowers for a second year, cut off the stems to about 8cm/4in above the pot when the leaves have fallen. Place it in a mild shady spot and let the compost dry off. In early May, water and repot. Keep watering and shoots will soon reappear. Feed regularly and prune the new growth to leave 4 or 5 strong stems.

Lighting then needs to be very carefully controlled from the end of September. The plant must be in complete darkness for 14 hours each day, so you must cover it with a black polythene bag or something similar. Do this for 8 weeks and then bring it into the light and start watering. Nursery men use a growth retardant to limit the size and bushiness of the poinsettia but this is not often on sale at garden centres.

CARE

Light and temperature
Bright light during winter and a minimum temperature of 13–15°C/55–60°F. The plant must be protected from hot summer sun if it is to flower again next Christmas.

Water and feeding
These plants need moist air, so spray frequently. Water well and wait until the compost is thoroughly dry before watering again. Water more liberally in summer or if leaves begin to wilt. Feed weekly from early summer to mid-autumn.

Propagation
Take a stem cutting in early summer. Using a rooting hormone powder, plant the cuttings in small peat pots in a propagator, having been treated in water to stem the milky white juices. They will take in 3 or 4 weeks.

Repotting
Pot on in fresh peat when new growth is evident. Keep the pot the same size to encourage flowering rather than leaf growth.

PROBLEMS

Red spider mite and mealy bug are the main pests and can be sprayed with insecticide.

Overwatering causes the leaves to fall off after wilting. Make sure the compost is dry before you water.

If the temperature is too low, or there is not enough light, leaves will fall without wilting.

Fuchsia

QUITE DIFFICULT

Fuchsia is one of the most popular flowering shrubs. Some hybrids can grow as tall as 2m/6ft outdoors, but inside the most suitable are dwarf or hanging varieties. There are certainly many to choose from, with flowers in almost every colour except yellow.

The plant blooms from March through to November, bearing highly ornamental bell-shaped flowers on stems that have small pointed deciduous leaves.

In summer, plants that are normally kept indoors will thrive if given short spells outside in bright light, but not direct sun. Buy small specimens in spring and place the pots in holders filled with wet gravel to increase humidity. In winter, though the leaves will drop, the plant will remain dormant if kept in a cool room.

Fuchsia's original habitat is New Zealand and Central America, where it grows to tree size in full sun.

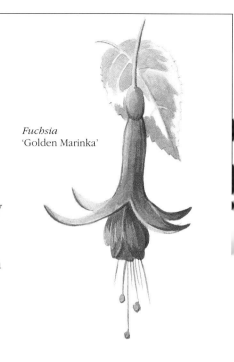

Fuchsia 'Golden Marinka'

Fuchsia 'Marinka', a red hanging type

Fuchsia 'Lena', one of
the many doubles

Fuchsia 'Winston Churchill', a single hybrid

CARE

Light and temperature
A bright position, but not full sun, with
temperatures of 15°C/60°F in summer
and 8–10°C/46–50°F in winter.

Water and feeding
Fuchsias like humidity, so spray often.
Water plentifully throughout flowering
and feed once a week. When the plants
are not in flower, feed each fortnight. In
winter allow the plant to dry out
between waterings.

Propagation
Cuttings from the tips can be rooted in
spring or autumn and set in a heated
propagator.

Repotting
As necessary, in a potting mixture made
of loam, peat and sand in equal parts.
Hanging varieties need to be pruned by
two-thirds in spring and repotted when
new shoots appear.

PROBLEMS

Aphids and whiteflies can infest the
plant. Spray with insecticide.

Leaves turn yellow and drop if the plant
becomes waterlogged. Allow to dry out
before watering again and ensure good
drainage.

Gloriosa rothschildiana (Glory lily, climbing lily, Mozambique lily)

EASY

Gloriosa rothschildiana is a tuber which originates from tropical East Africa and is part of the lily family. It is a vigorous climber, reaching over 2m/7ft in height, and in its native habitat it will quite happily clamber over other plants and trees. It has glossy leaves, the uppermost ones formed as tendrils which makes this an interesting plant even when the flowers are not out.

The stunning red flowers, veering towards orange at the base, have 6 petals with wavy edges that curve inwards. There are some entirely yellow varieties.

The plant blooms from June to August each year, but in a greenhouse can be forced to flower from February onwards. Rest periods are important. It should last a good few years – perhaps 6–8 – with the right conditions. The tubers contain poison.

It is a plant that is now becoming much more widely available.

CARE

Light and temperature
Gloriosa needs as much light and direct sunshine as possible. Its favourite temperature is 15–18°C/60–64°F. Protect the flowers from sun and scorching on very hot days.

Water and feeding
Water abundantly during growth and put the pot over a saucer of wet gravel. Feed with a weak solution of liquid fertilizer each fortnight. After flowering, allow the plant to dry out between each watering until it finally withers. Cut back all vegetation to just above soil level and cease watering. Place the pot in a dark spot and keep dry. Do not allow the temperature to drop below 8°C/48°F, then repot tubers into fresh compost in early spring.

Propagation
In early spring, separate the small tubers which have formed among the roots of the parent plant. These can be potted out and left to develop green buds at 15–18°C/60–64°F.

Repotting
Each year. In winter the parts of the plant above ground die off and the tubers should be kept at 10–12°C/50–54°F. In early spring repot these tubers in a mixture of loam, peat and sand mixed in equal parts. Each tuber will produce 3 stems, which need support.

PROBLEMS

Uneven temperatures and a drop in humidity may cause dark spots to appear on the leaves. Keep both constant.

Leaves may wilt if the temperature is too high.

If flowers fail to appear, move to a sunnier position and ensure the right degree of humidity.

Gloriosa rothschildiana is a climber with weak stems needing support. Also found is *Gloriosa superba* that has green and orange flowers fading to red.

Heliotropium arborescens (Heliotrope, cherry pie)

EASY

This flowering herb from Peru gives off a delicious vanilla scent from its tiny flowers which are borne on large heads. Its flowering season is throughout the summer, when the perfume can be easily and deliciously detected in any room. It is a simple plant to grow and can be trained as a standard.

In its native habitat and with sufficient humidity *Heliotropium* will grow into a large shrub. As an indoor plant it can reach up to 1m/3ft high and will live for many years, but it will lose its ability to produce flowers over time. The most commonly available are the purple varieties, but white- or blue-flowering heliotropes may be found.

CARE

Light and temperature
Plenty of light but no direct sun. Average warmth in summer and temperatures of not less than 8–10°C/40–50°F in winter.

Water and feeding
Keep the compost well watered in spring and summer but never allow the plant to become waterlogged. Feed at weekly intervals using a general liquid fertilizer to manufacturer's recommendations. Whilst dormant, allow the plant to dry out between waterings and do not feed.

Propagation
From seed in early spring or from cuttings taken in late spring or summer and rooted in seeding compost in a propagator at 21°C/70°F.

Repotting
Heliotropium thrives best if repotted each spring. Use a humus-rich compost and a pot one size larger.

PROBLEMS

Scale insects on the underside of leaves should be treated by using a swab dipped in methylated spirit.

Aphids can infest the plant. Spray with diluted malathion.

Thrips can cause the leaves to lose their colour and develop flecks. Spray with diluted malathion.

Heliotropum arborescens, sometimes known as *H. peruvianum* has attractively wrinkled leaves

Hibiscus rosa-sinensis (Chinese hibiscus)

EASY

Hibiscus plants look particularly pretty on windowsills where their large flowers with long yellow stamens can bloom almost continuously all summer.

   The trumpet-shaped flowers only last a day or two, but given the right care and attention you can achieve a succession of blooms over a few months. The flowers are large and measure up to 15cm/6in across. They can be double or single, in shades of yellow, orange, pink or red.

   In its native habitat of tropical Asia and Southern China, the plant grows up to 3m/10ft tall in full sunshine, but indoors generally it reaches a height of around 1m/3ft.

   Hibiscus can live for 20 years or more but needs to be pruned to keep it small and bushy. It can also be trained as a standard.

Hibiscus rosa-sinensis

CARE

Light and temperature
Very bright to full sun throughout summer. Warm temperatures during the flowering season. In winter, temperatures of around 15°C/60°F help promote the development of flowers in the next season.

Water and feeding
Water daily throughout summer until autumn, less in winter. From spring to autumn, feed each week; in winter, feed each month. *Hibiscus* must be fed otherwise it will not bloom.

Propagation
From top cuttings in late spring. Pot in fresh compost and keep moist and warm.

Repotting
Young plants need to be repotted each year. Older plants as necessary. Before repotting, cut back long shoots.

PROBLEMS

Dry compost will cause buds to drop.

Leaves will curl if the air is too dry.

Aphids and red spider mite can cause problems. Spray with insecticide.

Hippeastrum hybrids (Amaryllis, Barbados lily)

EASY

Clusters of glorious huge trumpet-shaped flowers in warm colours, from white through to scarlet-red, make *Hippeastrum* a dramatic sight and often there may be 2 flower stalks.

Many large bulbs are sold around Christmas time, specially prepared to come into bloom after around 5–6 weeks, from mid-winter to mid-spring. The bulbs have been forced, and will take up to a year to regain their strength and vigour.

The plant originates from tropical and subtropical America, but only hybridized forms are available today, mostly the result of Dutch breeders crossing *H. leopoldii* from Peru with other species. There are many different varieties: 'Apple Blossom' is sweet-smelling, pink and white; 'Ludwig's Goliath' is fiery red; 'Fantastica' is red-and-white striped and 'Fairyland' is pink. There are also other hybrids with stripes of 2 or 3 different colours.

Occasionally florists sell amaryllis as a cut flower, particularly in Europe; a bunch of pure white trumpets can look totally magical. 'Ludwig's Dazzler' is probably the best of the white varieties; others include 'Maria Goretti' and 'Early White'.

Parts of this plant are poisonous.

CARE

Light and temperature
The bulbs need a very bright and warm position to promote growth.

Water and feeding
Water very little until after growth begins. Once blooming has finished – around 3 weeks – allow the foliage and flower to die back (never cut this off) and keep feeding each week until late summer. This is necessary for the bulb to flower again the next year. In autumn, decrease watering and stop feeding, allowing the bulb a 3-month period of rest. Keep the bulb dry and warm until spring, or until new growth becomes evident.

Propagation
This requires considerable effort from the home gardener, but the truly dedicated can separate side bulbs the size of marbles from the mother bulb, or sow seeds. Generally speaking, it is best to buy fresh bulbs, which will flower for 2 or 3 years and should then be discarded.

Repotting
Plant overwintered bulbs in a roomy pot with good compost every 2 years. Half the bulb must show above the soil. Remove 3cm/1in of topsoil and replace with fresh compost each spring. Always use a mixture of bonemeal and composted leaves with garden soil, rather than peat-based compost, which weakens the bulb.

PROBLEMS

Fire disease can attack the bulb, in which case it should be discarded before the rest of the stock becomes infected.

If the plant fails to produce new leaves or flower stalks it may have been too cold or wet at a critical stage. Move to a warmer site and follow watering instructions.

Leaf tips turning yellow are a sign of overwatering. Cut back on frequency.

Leaf scorch, a fungal disease, can eat at the bulb. Infected areas can be cut out and the bulb dusted with charcoal if the signs are spotted in time. If not, discard immediately.

Hippeastrum 'Red Lion'

Kalanchoe blossfeldiana (Flaming Katie, Palm Beach belle)

EASY

Kalanchoe blossfeldiana is the most commonly found variety of this succulent, and indeed perhaps the most commonly sold houseplant. In its native Madagascar its bright red flowers appear during the winter, though Dutch breeders have manipulated hybrids which flower throughout the year, in colours from yellow and orange to pink and purple. It will appreciate a spell out of doors in a sunny sheltered spot in summer months, and can reach a height of 30cm/12in, though dwarf varieties are sometimes seen for sale.

Kalanchoe manginii is a spring-flowering type, demanding higher humidity, so stand on a tray of moist gravel and mist the leaves frequently. The flowers hang downwards, making good display of this plant important. 'Wendy' and 'Tessa' are just two of the many hybrids available.

CARE

Light and temperature
An east- or west-facing windowsill from spring to autumn and a south-facing windowsill in winter. It needs average warmth, with a minimum 10°C/50°F in winter. Remember these plants only develop flowers when they receive 8–10 hours of light each day for 4–6 weeks.

Water and feeding
Use high-potash fertilizer every 4 weeks during spring and summer. Water very sparingly during winter.

Propagation
Mostly done from seed sown in March or April. Leaf cuttings or whole shoots can be taken in spring and summer. Use a sharp knife and dust with hormone rooting powder. Either lay leaves or insert stems into a sand and peat compost.

Repotting
Best to do this straight after flowering if retaining the plant for a further season's flowering.

PROBLEMS

White woolly patches on leaves are caused by mealy bug. Remove with a methylated spirit swab.

Black patches on leaves can be removed by dusting the flowers with sulphur.

Wet and cold conditions cause leaves to drop and stems to become black. Dry the plant out.

Right: *Kalanchoe manginii* 'Tessa'

The fleshy leaves of *Kalanchoe* look a rich reddy-green in sunlight

Lantana (Yellow sage, shrub verbena)

QUITE EASY

Originating in the West Indies, this plant grows up to 2m/6ft and is a vigorous and fast-growing shrub, flowering throughout the year if it has sufficient light. Only dwarf hybrids are cultivated for indoor use. If left untrimmed, *Lantana* will reach 1.2m/4ft, but it is best pruned into a smaller, bushier shape. It can look good in a hanging basket.

It has pretty white, pink or yellow tubular flowers, which darken with age, on prickly stems that have rough leaves. It will bloom between May and October, but the only reliable indoor cultivar is *Lantana hybrida* 'Nana'. It should be discarded after 3–4 years.

CARE

Light and temperature
Lots of sunlight – it will not flower unless it gets 3–4 hours of direct sun each day throughout the year. It likes good air circulation and copes well with summer room temperatures. Rest in winter at about 10°C/50°F.

Water and feeding
Water freely while in flower and feed with liquid fertilizer each fortnight. In winter, allow the compost almost to dry out between waterings.

Propagation
From 10cm/4in cuttings taken from a non-flowering branch in August. Strip off the leaves, dip in rooting powder and plant in a mixture of peat and sand. Place in a greenhouse at 18°C/64°F, in bright but filtered light. Leave the cuttings over winter. In early spring, pinch the tips to encourage a bushy shape. In March, pot into standard growing soil.

Repotting
When potbound in compost made up of organic soil, sand and peat.

PROBLEMS

Lantana is very prone to whitefly. Spray with insecticide.

Lantana hybrida 'Nana'

Leptospermum scoparium (Tea tree, Manuka)

EASY

Leptospermum grow to form small upright bushes

CARE

Light and temperature
Requires full sun all year round and likes at least 6–8 hours of daylight. You may need artificial light during the winter months.
Winter temperatures can be those of an unheated greenhouse but never subject the plant to frost.

Water and feeding
Use soft rain water, preferably at room temperature. Lime is abhorrent to the plant. Keep the compost moist throughout the flowering season and in winter water sparingly, allowing the compost to dry out between waterings. Feed on a fortnightly basis during the flowering season.

Propagation
New growth can be potted on in spring, or after flowering more mature cuttings can be dipped in hormone rooting powder. Use a mixture of humus-rich compost and sand. Plants should take root in 6 weeks.

Repotting
Each spring the tea tree should be moved into a pot one size larger. Use a rich houseplant compost.

PROBLEMS

If the flower buds fail to form, increase the dose of liquid fertilizer and ensure that the compost does not dry out.

Occasionally aphids will attack this plant. Make sure that it has sufficient air circulation.

The tea tree is a subtropical plant native to Australia and New Zealand where it climbs to 6m/20ft, using other vegetation as a means of support. The extraordinary thing about this plant is the fragrant oil glands in the leaves. There are masses of flowers, which in many ways resemble roses, on the upright foliage. In some species these may be white and in others pinkish. The plant will flower from late spring until the beginning of autumn.

L. s. 'Album' has bigger flowers, with equally silky foliage, and *L. s.* 'Ruby Glow' has crimson flowers in considerable profusion. There are both single- and double-flowered varieties and some forms have deep bronze leaves. The leaves of all varieties have very sharp tips.

It is possible to keep *Leptospermum* going for a number of years, but judicious pruning at the onset of spring is helpful.

Lilium (Lily)

Lilium

EASY

These types of lilies come mostly from China or other parts of South East Asia, where they grow in a warm and temperate climate. The glorious blooms and scent can last for up to 3 weeks indoors.

Lilies are bulbs and it is important to buy plump firm bulbs with no signs of wrinkling or softness. The autumn is the best time to plant them. Until growth begins, they need to be kept cool, dark and moist, then, when growth starts, they can be moved to a brighter position. All lilies need to be staked otherwise their tall stems can easily topple.

There are 3 main types of lily:

Turk's Cap-shaped lilies – swept back petals with small flowers. Popular varieties include *L. citronella*, which produces yellow flowers with black dots in summer and reaches 90cm/3ft high, with 10cm/3in flowers. *L. fiesta* hybrids are taller, reaching 1m/3ft.

Trumpet-shaped lilies – also flower in summer. *L. longiflorum eximium* (Easter or Madonna lily) has fragrant white flowers 12cm/5in across. There is a 'Mt Everest' variety.

L. regale (regal lily) bears white flowers with yellow throats and has a powerful scent. The yellow variety is 'Royal Gold'. There is a group all reaching the 1.1m/4ft mark, called the 'Mid-century' hybrids, dramatically coloured with medium-sized flowers appearing in early summer. Varieties included 'Brandywine', 'Cinnabar', 'Destiny', 'Enchantment' and 'Prosperity'.

Bowl-shaped lilies – flared petals opening to produce a wide bowl. These include *L. auratum* (goldband lily) and *L. speciosum* (Japanese Lily).

Consider lilies as annuals when grown indoors. The bulbs have been specially treated to force them into flower. Plant them in the garden after the blooms have faded and the foliage has shrivelled.

CARE

Light and temperature
In winter, prepare the pot with charcoal at the bottom for good drainage, overlaid with sphagnum moss and bulb fibre or a sandy soil. Bury the bulbs with at least 3cm/1in compost above their heads. Set the pot in a dark frost-free place with the temperature at around 4°C/40°F. Move to a warmer, better lit spot when growth begins in spring. Gradually give more light and warmth, eventually providing bright light, but no direct sun.

When the flower fades and the stalks yellow, allow the plant to die down completely before planting outside in the garden in a sandy, humus-rich soil.

Water and feeding
During the growing season water well but never let the bulb become waterlogged. Reduce watering to allow bulb to dry off after flowering.

Propagation
Difficult. Best left to a professional.

Repotting
Plant on into a garden.

PROBLEMS

Overwatering and bad drainage can lead to rot. Yellowing flower tips are a sign of this. Allow the plant to dry out as fast as possible.

If grey mould appears on new growth as the plant develops, the ventilation is insufficient and should be improved. A dusting with sulphur will help.

L. speciosum rubrum   *L. auratum*

Medinilla magnifica (Rose grape)

DIFFICULT

As the common name suggests, from March to June this bushy plant bears arching stems of drooping rose-pink flowers shaped like bunches of grapes and set in sensationally pretty pink bracts. The pairs of leaves have no stalks and measure up to 30cm/12in long and 12cm/5in wide. The stem of the plant is woody and has many branches.

Its native habitat is the tropical jungles of the Philippines, where it was discovered in 1888. There it grows to 2.5m/8ft, but as an indoor plant it reaches no more than 1m/3ft. It is difficult to make a success of indoors because it needs controlled temperature and humidity levels. Thus it is expensive. It is also best suited to a conservatory where it should last for a good number of years.

Medinilla magnifica

CARE

Light and temperature
In summer, it needs bright light but no direct sun. In winter it can take direct sunlight. It needs high temperatures of 18–27°C/64–80°F in summer. In winter it can tolerate 15–18°C/60–64°F when the plant is at rest, which is essential for further flowering.

Water and feeding
Water moderately, letting the soil almost dry out between waterings. In winter, water less. Humidity needs to be high and the foliage sprayed each day. The plant should be placed in a saucer of wet gravel. Feed with liquid fertilizer each fortnight from when buds form until September.

Propagation
Leave to the professionals.

Repotting
Every other spring in a compost made up of leaf mould, sphagnum moss, peat and sand. Pinch out tips of stems to encourage branching.

PROBLEMS

Prone to red spider mite. Spray with diluted malathion.

If flowers do not form, increase the difference in seasonal treatments, giving higher, more humid conditions in spring and cooler temperatures in the rest period.

Mimosa pudica (Sensitive plant, humbleplant)

QUITE EASY

This small shrub from the tropical areas of Brazil grows like a weed in the wild and is a different genus from the yellow-flowered mimosa sold by florists. *Mimosa pudica* has pom-pom flowers which bloom from July through to September, and feathery leaves like an ash tree. The leaf axils are also hairy.

The plant loses its beauty as it ages and because of this it is usually cultivated as an annual and discarded after flowering.

It is an extremely reactive plant, hence its common name. The small leaves will fold up tightly if they are touched or if the plant is shaken, and similarly if subjected to heat from a lighted candle or cigarette. The stalks may also droop. If left alone for about 30 minutes, the leaves will gradually unfold and the stems straighten. This behaviour only occurs during the daytime and it is thought that heat is the trigger.

The plant needs high humidity, having been adapted for the house from a plant found on the constantly moist forest floor. It grows from seed to a height of about 60cm/2ft.

CARE

Light and temperature
It needs bright light and direct sun (though not midday sun) for 3–4 hours each day. It does best at normal room temperatures of 18–22°C/64–71°F.

Water and feeding
Mimosa pudica needs high humidity, so place the plant over a saucer of wet gravel. Allow the soil to dry out before watering and feed with liquid fertilizer each fortnight while the plant is in bloom.

Propagation
Sow seed in February or March, 2–3 seeds to each 8cm/3in pot. Keep in bright filtered light at 18–20°C/64–68°F. Water sparingly and keep only the strongest seedling when it reaches 4–5cm/2in.

Repotting
Discard after flowering.

PROBLEMS

Failure to flower is caused by not enough humidity. Place in a position that has better light and ensure the tray of pebbles is sufficiently moist at all times.

Mimosa pudica

Musa cavendishii (Dwarf banana plant, dwarf ladyfinger banana)

EASY

Musa cavendishii

This plant, also known as *Musa nana*, was named after Antonium Musa, doctor to Octavius Augustus, the first Emperor of Rome, as it was first brought back from the tropical areas of southern China by Roman troops. It was introduced into England in 1849. Smaller varieties were very popular with Victorian gardeners, who favoured the plant for their conservatories. It is cultivated commercially in the Canary Islands and Florida and can be grown successfully indoors in a well-lit position.

In its native, tropical habitat, the plant bears fruit and grows to a height of 12m/40ft or more. Indoors, it will still produce edible fruit but will reach only 1.8m/6ft, with dramatic leaves up to 1m/3ft long.

As the fruit is seedless, the banana must be propagated from suckers. These grow quickly, often as much as 60cm/2ft a year. Take great care with the leaves as they are delicate and can be easily torn. Plants only last 4–5 years.

CARE

Light and temperature
Place in strong light and normal room temperature, with a minimum winter temperature of 15°C/60°F.

Water and feeding
Water liberally in summer, every 10 days in winter. Feed in summer each fortnight with liquid food and provide rich compost. Place the pot on wet pebbles and spray often, but make sure that there is no surplus water on the leaves as this will cause scorching if the plant is in direct sunlight.

Propagation
This plant is seedless and can only be propagated by splitting suckers from the adult plant in spring and potting on in high temperatures (21–27°C/70–80°F) and humidity.

Repotting
Every spring, using fresh compost.

PROBLEMS

White woolly patches in the axils of leaves indicate mealy bug. Remove with a swab dipped in methylated spirit.

If the trunk appears to rot the plant is breaking down due to overwatering and low temperature. Raise the temperature and dust the flowers with sulphur.

Nerium oleander (Oleander, rose bay)

DIFFICULT

The oleander is native to the whole Mediterranean region, where in summer it blooms almost continuously. It grows on sunny slopes and rocky hillsides to a height of 3m/20ft as a dense bushy shrub covered with white, pink, peach, red and yellow flowers. The leaves are a lovely silvery green and the flowers can have a delightful fragrance.

When this plant is cultivated for indoors, it generally reaches about 60cm/2ft and flowers only during July and August. It needs full sun. A variegated variety is to be found occasionally.

The whole plant is extremely poisonous – men have died from drinking liquid stirred with an oleander twig – so keep well away from children. It needs pruning once flowering is over; be sure to wash your hands thoroughly after touching it.

PROBLEMS

Prone to attacks by scale insects. Spray with insecticide.

If no flower buds develop, increase the light and hours of sunshine if possible. Make sure there is good ventilation too.

CARE

Light and temperature
It needs direct sun and is best placed outdoors during summer, where strong light will help promote flowering. Indoors it lives at summer room temperature, provided it has strong direct light each day. In winter temperatures can drop to 12–14°C/53–57°F. It can stand temperatures as low as 8°C/46°F, but will not tolerate frosts. The oleander is not a lover of heating systems.

Water and feeding
In summer, water moderately, letting the soil surface dry out between waterings. Given the sun it craves this could mean watering daily. Do not allow the roots to dry out or the flower buds will fall before opening. In winter, reduce watering. Feed with a weak liquid fertilizer each fortnight between May and September or one that has a high nitrogen content.

Propagation
From 15cm/6in cuttings taken from non-flowering shoots in June. Root these in water and transfer into good compost when they begin to show growth. The cuttings can also be rooted into a mixture of peat and sand.

Repotting
Every spring, with fresh soil.

Nerium oleander

Nertera granadensis (Bead plant, coral bead plant, baby tears)

QUITE EASY

This member of the madder family is a curious-looking but attractive low-growing creeping plant. Its fleshy green leaves intertwine to form a thick mat, with the whole plant growing no more than 7–8cm/3in high. Small white flowers are produced in June, followed by orangy-red berries covering the entire plant. These berries fall after a few months, and there are often so many of them that the foliage is hidden.

The native habitat of the bead plant stretches from the Andes to Cape Horn, New Zealand and Tasmania. It grows in high mountain zones at least 2000m/6500ft above sea level and so requires a lot of direct sunlight.

The plant is low, and should be grown in a container where the decorative berries can be displayed well.

CARE

Light and temperature
Needs 3–4 hours of direct sun a day, so a south-facing windowsill is ideal. However it requires cool temperatures of between 14–17°C/57–62°F. The plant will become straggly and refuse to bear fruit if it is placed in rooms which lack light or are too warm.

Water and feeding
Water thoroughly as needed, but let the surface soil dry out before repeating. Place the plant in a saucer of wet gravel. In winter reduce watering, but do not allow the plant to become completely dry. Feed only once a month, when the berries begin forming.

Propagation
In spring, divide clumps of old plants into 5 or 6 small portions and repot individually into fresh soil made up of peat, sand and organic mulch.

Repotting
Repot each year in spring when dividing.

PROBLEMS

Do not over-fertilize, or you will promote leaf growth rather than flowering.

If the flowers open but berries fail to form move to a better ventilated position.

Nertera granadensis is also sometimes sold as *Nertera depressa*.

Orchid phalaenopsis (Moth orchid)

DIFFICULT

These demanding plants are quite stunning during their long flowering period, which can last almost throughout the year. Several flower spikes can follow on after each other and the arching stalks carry many blooms. It is a pseudobulb, with fleshy light green leaves.

Many people fail with the moth orchid because it is very difficult to emulate the conditions in which the plant grows in its native habitat of Malaya.

A constant temperature is required – in summer 25°C/70°F and 16°C/60°F in winter. A cool night temperature helps. The difficulty of keeping the moth orchid at home is providing 10–15 hours light each day, so artificial light in winter is essential. The plants need no rest period. They can last for 4–5 years with the right care.

PROBLEMS

If the leaves shrivel and rot at the stem this may be caused by overwatering. Allow compost to dry out and reduce future waterings.

If the plant fails to produce new flower stalks, the most likely cause is insufficient light and humidity. Use artificial light if necessary and increase humidity.

Greenfly may attack this plant. Use insecticide before infestation becomes too serious.

CARE

Light and temperature
High temperatures by day and cooler at night is the secret of success with this plant. Place in a warm spot with as much daylight, but no direct sun, as you can manage.

Water and feeding
Humid conditions help enormously; stand the plant over a tray of damp pebbles if at all possible and spray the leaves often. Water weekly during flowering, ensuring the plant has good drainage.

Propagation
The moth orchid produces side bulbs, which may be separated from the parent plant. Remove the plant from the pot and delicately sort out the roots, washing thoroughly. Cut the bulb away if necessary with a sharp knife and pot up into specially prepared orchid compost which has been pre-moistened. The growth should start in 3–4 weeks. Water sparingly during that time.

Repotting
Only when absolutely essential if the plant is potbound, every 2 years or so. Use a special orchid compost, rich in sphagnum moss and osmunda fibre.

Osteospermum (Trailing African daisy, Burgundy mound)

EASY

In its native habitat of the Cape and Natal province of South Africa, *Osteospermum* grows as ground cover and spreads easily. In the last year or so Danish nursery men have hybridized an indoor variety which is now marketed successfully throughout the summer months.

Its leaves have several points and are smallish. The cheerful flowers are a delicate purple fading to white on the upper side, with a deeper purple colour on the underside of the petals, the centres are dark purple. A most attractive and unusual plant, the flowering season lasts for 2 to 3 months. A white variety, *Osteospermum fruticosum* 'Album' is occasionally found on sale.

Osteospermum throws out long trailing branches which root easily, and can be cut and planted to increase stock. The plant will last for a couple of years but then loses vigour and is best replaced.

CARE

Light and temperature
Normal room temperature is fine; keep plant on a sunny, south-facing windowsill if possible, and give plenty of light during the winter months. Artificial light is not necessary.

Water and feeding
Keep the compost moist, but provide good drainage. Weekly watering in the winter rest period should be sufficient. Feed with a weak solution of houseplant fertilizer on a 7-day basis when in bud and flowering.

Propagation
Use the plantlets from the trailers and pot up into moist compost in spring. Water sparingly until new growth is obvious, then treat as a mature plant. Three or four months later flowering should commence.

Repotting
In early spring, into ordinary houseplant compost. Use a pot 1 size larger. This should only be necessary if trying to keep plant for a second season. Otherwise discard.

PROBLEMS

Whitefly needs to be treated with insecticide.

If plant becomes leggy, pinch out growing tips to encourage flowering and bushiness.

Osteospermum fruticosum

199

Ruellia (Monkey plant, trailing velvet plant)

Ruellia makoyana

DIFFICULT

Ruellia makoyana, a pretty native of Brazil, has glorious carmine trumpet-shaped flowers and velvety leaves with silver veins and purple edges. The oval leaves are particularly subtle and beautiful, with the plant flowering in late autumn and early winter.

The species was named after Jean de la Ruells, who was both botanist and physician to Francis I of France in the sixteenth century, and grows in its native habitat in high humidity under a semi-shade canopy.

Ruellia macrantha (Christmas pride) again has carmine flowers and is somewhat larger; however the leaves do not have the attractive veining of *Ruellia makoyana*.

In the home you should be able to keep these plants going for 2 or 3 years. Pinch out growing tips to encourage bushiness. Both can be used in hanging baskets.

Ruellia makoyana
flower and leaf

CARE

Light and temperature
Bright indirect sunlight with an average summer household temperature. Do not let it go above 21°C/70°F and, at this temperature, you should provide plenty of humidity by placing the plant on pebbles in a saucer of water. This is not really a plant for heated rooms. During winter do not let the temperature drop below 13°C/55°F.

Water and feeding
During spring and summer water well, but wait until the surface of the soil has dried out between waterings. Feed fortnightly with general liquid fertilizer to the manufacturer's recommendations. In winter water weekly but do not fertilize.

Repotting
Repot in early autumn in a loam-based compost and add granules.

Propagation
Take stem-tip cuttings with 4 pairs of leaves in summer and root into potting mixture. Place in a propagator but ventilate once a day.

PROBLEMS

Greenfly insects can cover the leaves and growing points. Spray with diluted malathion. Also spray with diluted malathion if whiteflies jump around the plant.

Whitish mould on the leaves and stems can be caused by botrytis, or stem rot. The plant is too wet and cold. Spray with fungicide and move to a warmer position.

Webs under the leaves are caused by red spider mite. Spray with a systemic insecticide. Water the plant thoroughly and spray over the leaves frequently to increase humidity.

If leaves turn black, the location is too cold. Move the plant to a warmer position.

If the leaves shrivel up, the plant is too dry or too hot. Check the compost and water if dry. If the compost is moist enough, move the plant to a cooler spot.

Schizanthus retusus (Butterfly flower, poor man's orchid)

EASY

Only hybrids of the butterfly flower from Chile are available; there it grows as an annual in subtropical conditions in full sunshine to a height of 1m/3ft. Cultivated as an indoor plant, it remains an annual and should be bought in bud, to be discarded after flowering, which can last 4 or 5 months until late autumn.

The foliage is gracefully fernlike, the stems of the plant being somewhat sticky. The flowers look similar to those of the orchid and are around 5cm/2in wide, coming most commonly in a salmon-pink colour with a yellow centre on which there are purple markings. Other colour bands include bright red, purple and pink varieties, *S. x wisetonensis* hybrids, again with yellow centres marked with purple.

Both dwarf and larger varieties can easily be grown from seed. If sown in spring it produces autumn-flowering plants, and if in autumn spring blossoms.

A good plant for hanging baskets, the tips of the growing specimen should be pinched out to encourage bushiness.

Schizanthus needs good air circulation and bright light to do well

PROBLEMS

If foliage begins to look dry and flower buds fail to open, increase watering. Make sure you protect the plant from potential sun scorch.

CARE

Light and temperature
Full light. South-facing window boxes and hanging baskets are ideal. Keep at cool or average warmth – 13–18°C/55–64°F is best.

Water and feeding
Keep the soil moist, but not wet. Feed each fortnight with liquid fertilizer until flowering has finished.

Propagation
Sow seed either in spring or autumn. Pinch out tips of young plants to encourage bushy growth.

Repotting
Not necessary as the plant is an annual.

Schlumbergera (Thanksgiving cactus, Christmas cactus, claw cactus)

QUITE EASY

In its natural habitat of tropical Brazil, this member of the cactus family is epiphytic, attaching itself on to trees that grow on mountains up to 1500m/4800ft.

Forced by hybridizing and the treatment meted out by nursery men, it is a strikingly attractive plant growing to about 30cm/1ft, and has stems formed of flat joints with a few well-marked 'teeth'. The flowers appear in winter and, for a cactus, are long-lasting – maybe 3 or 4 days. They are usually pink, but modern hybrids include white, red, yellow and purple varieties.

S. bridgesii is the Christmas cactus and *S. truncata* (sometimes known as *Zygocactus truncatus*) the Thanksgiving cactus, also called the claw cactus. They both come into flower in early November and can last for 50 years or more.

Schlumbergera bridgesii looks extremely handsome in a hanging basket or against plain terracotta pots.

CARE

Light and temperature
Some direct sun all year round. It does fine at room temperature. An abundance of flowers can be encouraged by keeping the plant out of artificial light for long periods during early autumn when buds are setting. An outdoor spell is recommended – a shady protected position in summer.

Water and feeding
Keep the soil moist but not wet, using rain water if possible. When flowering finishes, reduce the amount of water. Use high-potassium fertilizer every fortnight all year round except in the 2 months after flowering.

Propagation
In spring take cuttings of 2 to 3 joints, let the surface dry out and pot into a humus-rich compost. Rooting occurs in about 3 or 4 weeks.

Repotting
In spring, but only when roots fill the container. Use a mixture of leaf compost, soil, peat and sand, and keep dryish for the first 2 weeks.

PROBLEMS

Scale insects and mealy bug may infest the plant. Spray with insecticide.

If the plant shrivels up, it has probably been kept too dry. Increase watering and keep the compost moist.

If flowers fail to appear, the plant has been kept too warm during the rest period. Increase contrast in temperature and ensure 2 months' rest for the plant.

Senecio cruentis hybridus (Florists' cineraria)

QUITE EASY

This plant comes in almost every colour imaginable except yellow. It grows to 60cm/2ft and is covered with masses of small daisy-shaped flowers in early spring. There are dwarf, single and double varieties available, but the doubles are limited in their range of colours and will flower less freely. Buy plants with a few open flowers and plenty of buds; the flowering season lasts up to 2 months.

Senecio cruentis is very popular with parks departments for display purposes and is a good conservatory plant, preferring cool temperatures and little direct sun.

Its original habitat is the Canary Islands, where it grows as a half-hardy perennial, high up on the damp mountainsides in cool conditions. As a houseplant, it should be discarded after flowering.

Cineraria likes to have plenty of air circulation and humidity

Two of the many colour variations of singles   Double   Stellata

PROBLEMS

Yellow leaves are caused by draughty conditions. Move the plant to a more protected position.

Wilting leaves and drooping flowers are caused by the plant being either too dry and hot or overwatered. Resite the plant and reduce watering.

Flowers die prematurely if the plant is underwatered or receives too much sunlight.

CARE

Light and temperature.
Cinerarias like cool temperatures between 13°C/55°F. A north-facing windowsill is ideal. Keep out of direct sun, which will cause the plants to wilt and they will never recover completely.

Water and feeding
Water, then allow to dry out. Take care not to overwater and ensure good drainage. Feeding is not necessary as this only produces coarse plants with excessively sized leaves.

Propagation
From seed in summer, but earlier sowings will produce plants that bloom in midwinter. Do not bury the fine seed, but cover with glass or polythene. When the seedlings appear, spray them often, pot up in September and keep in an unheated greenhouse. When buds appear, raise the temperature to 13°C/55°F.

Repotting
Not necessary; plants are discarded after flowering.

Streptocarpus (Cape primrose)

EASY

The delicate *Streptocarpus* or Cape primrose, which as its name suggests comes from subtropical Southern Africa, was brought to Europe in the 1820s. It grows naturally in humid, leafy shaded soil, often clinging to rocky surfaces, and can cope with semi-shaded conditions within the home.

Recently plant breeders have produced a range of hybrids. Purple or mauve is still the predominant colour, and 'Constant Nymph' the old favourite, but there are many different shades within this spectrum, from the deep purple of 'Amanda' to the soft mauve petals and darker throat stripes of 'Heidi'. White, pink and red varieties are also found.

Other varieties include the pretty mauve *Streptocarpus saxorum*, which can be trained into an attractive hanging plant, and the extraordinary *Streptocarpus wenlandii* with only one enormous leaf, that is red underneath.

The plant flowers twice a year and will live for 2 to 3 years before it needs replacing. After flowering cut the stems at the base to encourage new flower shoots. Mature plants grow to a height of 30cm/12in.

PROBLEMS

Streptocarpus is vulnerable to remarkably few pests and diseases. Give it the conditions outlined and it will thrive.

Shrivelled leaves suggest the plant is too dry. Increase watering.

Droopy leaves again indicate it is too dry. Increase watering.

Leaf stems may rot if the plant is too wet and too cold. Water less and move to a warmer place. Dusting with sulphur may help.

Prone to greenfly. These tend to attack the flower stems rather than the leaves or flowers themselves. Spray with insecticide. The stems may also be attacked by thrips; treat in the same way.

'Falling Stars'   'Stella'

'Heidi'   'Amanda'

CARE

Light and temperature
Streptocarpus is a remarkably tolerant plant in most respects, but it does need plenty of light. Protect it from direct sunlight in summer. The ideal temperature is 16–18°C/63–67°F.

Water and feeding
Water 2–3 times a week in summer, but do not let the plant stand in water. In centrally heated rooms, increase the humidity by placing the pot in damp pebbles. Good drainage is vital. It does not require much feeding – a half-strength dose once every two weeks is plenty.

Repotting
Repot every spring in peat-based compost into a pot one size up. *Streptocarpus* likes fresh soil even if it doesn't need more space, so replace the top 2.5cm/1in of soil.

Propagation
They are easy to propagate. Leaf cuttings should be taken in summer. Cut a leaf along the central vein, cover the cut with rooting hormone and plant the cut surface in sharp sand.

Thunbergia alata (Black-eyed Susan)

EASY

This is one of the most effective flowering climbers, suitable for covering a trellis or being trained in a hanging basket for a conservatory or garden room. It has orange, yellow or white flowers with dark purple centres, and pale green serrated leaves.

Its native habitat is subtropical East Africa, where it grows to 4m/10ft. As an indoor plant it is unlikely to exceed 2.5m/6ft.

It can cover a large area very quickly but must have support. It is often treated as an annual but is actually a perennial which can be kept going for 2 or 3 years. After flowering, cut back the growth to 15cm/6in above soil level, fertilize regularly and repot in early springtime.

Thunbergia alata

CARE

Light and temperature
The plant needs some direct sun to flower successfully and should ideally be placed on a sunny terrace after flowering finishes, at the end of summer, until the frost arrives. Room temperature is adequate. Good air circulation is important.

Water and feeding
Regular watering throughout the flowering period should be cut back through the winter with the compost kept just moist. Mist from time to time and feed with liquid fertilizer each fortnight during flowering.

Propagation
Sow seeds in spring to flower through summer.

Repotting
In early spring into a humus-rich compost.

PROBLEMS

The leaves will shrivel easily if the plant is underwatered.

If flowerbuds fail to appear in the second season, increase fertilizing and move to a sunnier spot.

photosynthesis The action of light on the chlorophyll in the leaves, which converts the carbon dioxide that has been absorbed by the plant from the atmosphere into carbohydrate (food)

pinch out The removal of the growing tip, either by cutting or pinching off with the fingers, to encourage bushiness and/or flowering. (See page 240.)

pinnae Leaflets, or sub-sections, of a pinnate leaf

pinnate A compound leaf structure, with pairs of leaflets (pinnae) arranged opposite each other along the stalk

pistil The collective name for the ovary, style and stigma – the female reproductive parts of the plant

plantlet see *offset*

potbound A plant whose roots have filled the pot, therefore having no room for further growth

potting on Moving a plant into a larger size pot

powdery mildew A fungal disease which coats leaves with a white, powdery deposit. (See page 245.)

pricking out Transplanting seedlings into larger containers or individual pots

propagation Multiplying plants to increase supply or to replenish old stock. Can be achieved in a number of ways, e.g. by seed, by division, from leaf cutting, from stem cutting or from offsets. (See page 238.)

propagator Piece of equipment that provides the right conditions for propagating seeds and cuttings, i.e. warmth and a moist atmosphere. Can range from just a plastic dome over a seed tray to the electrical kind which provides and controls heat

pseudobulb The swollen base of the stem of an orchid with leaves and flowers. Used to store water, and often found growing from a rhizome

raceme A type of inflorescence – a central stem along which are spaced flowers on short stalks. Flowers usually bloom from the bottom upwards

red spider mite Sap-sucking, 8-legged insect noticible from black dots of excreta on leaves. (See page 245.)

repotting Removing a plant from its container, discarding topsoil and pruning roots, then replacing in same pot with fresh topsoil. (See page 242.)

rest period see *dormancy period*

rhizome A thick-stemmed storage organ, found either underground or lying on the surface. May have roots, leaves and flowering stems. (See also *bulb, tuber.*)

rootball The clump of roots and compost in the pot

rosette Arrangement of leaves spreading out from the central base of the plant

scale insect Sap-sucking pest usually attacking underside of leaf. Ferns and citrus plants are particularly vulnerable. (See page 245.)

scorching The burning of leaves or petals by the rays of the sun through a window

seed Fertilized ovule of a flowering plant, from which germinates a new plant

seedling The young plant sprouting from the seed

shrub Woody-stemmed plant which is smaller than a tree and has no trunk

single flower Flower which has only one row of petals. Many species have single and double varieties. (See also *double flower.*)

spadix A tongue-like flower spike, protruding from or surrounded by a spathe, for example as found on *Anthurium*

spathe A large, prominent bract bearing or surrounding a spadix

species Sub-division of a plant genus, written after genus name, e.g. *Celosia cristata, Celosia plumosa.* (See also *family, genus, variety.*)

sphagnum A young moss, with a very high air-filled porosity, used in potting mixes

spike A type of inflorescence – stalkless flowers growing alternately up a central stem

spore Minute seed of the fern family

stalk Arm of plant which bears the leaves and flower or flowers

stamen Pollen-bearing lobes or anthers – the male reproductive parts of the flower

stigma The point on the flower where fertilization occurs. Coated with a slippery substance, it is the upper part of the pistil and vital in the reproductive system

style The stalk of the female reproductive system, it supports the stigma and connects it to the ovary

succulent Used to describe indoor plants with thick and fleshy leaves. Often found growing natively in dry desert-like conditions where rainfall is short. Some have the ability to store moisture in their leaves; others can tolerate a little rain

systemic Usually refers to a pesticide taken from the leaves into the plant via the sap flow (or vascular system)

tendril A spiralling growth which some climbing plants use to attach themselves as a means of support. Tendrils are usually far finer than the stems from which they grow; some are grown from the leaves and others from the stems of the plants

terrarium Glass growing units for small plants which need high humidity. Also called Wardian cases after the botanist who invented them. Today's versions come with all services such as heat, humidity and ventilation

thrip Minute black insect which either flies or jumps to spread its influence, distorting flowers and leaves as it goes. (See page 245.)

throat The inner areas of a flower from which protrude the anther, filament and eye. Usually a different colour from the petals

transpiration Although it varies with the prevailing conditions, transpiration measures the loss of water vapour through the pores in the leaf structure. Transpiration (evaporation) increases with higher temperatures

tuber Storage root, usually underground. It is fleshy, and may seem thickened. From it grow leaf structures from which buds are borne. Important in the propagation of certain plants

umbel A type of inflorescence – a cluster of flowers, either flat or rounded, which arise from the same point, such as found on *Hoya bella*

variegated Two- (or more) coloured leaves. The white or yellow markings are patches that contain no green chlorophyll, be they in the form of stripes, leaf edges or flecks. Therefore the plants should be placed in good light to increase assimilation wherever possible. Chlorophyll is stored in this way and essential to healthy development

variety A sub-division of a plant species, written in inverted commas, e.g. *Leptospermum scoparium* 'Album', *Leptospermum scoparium* 'Ruby Glow'. May sometimes be called a cultivar. Usually indicates differences in size, colour or other features (See also *family, genus, variety.*)

white fly A sap-sucking, small white winged pest that clusters on the underside of plant leaves. (See page 244.)

whorl Three flowers or leaves which grow from the same node (or point) and radiate like the spokes of a wheel

Temperature

Plants survive a remarkably wide range of temperatures but what can be fatal is fluctuation of heat. Plants will withstand short periods in temperatures either too high or too low, but in the long term will die.

The right room temperature
The first stage is to consider the temperatures in which *you* want to live, and to select plants that will tolerate those temperatures. The vast range of plants do well with normal heat, given of course that other conditions such as light and humidity are also well suited to their needs. Most plants will tolerate a maximum temperature of 24°C/75°F and minimum of 10°C/50°F. During rest periods for certain groups lower temperatures are preferred, usually during the winter months – down to conditions in which one would not wish to live, such as 10°C/50°F.

Temperature and humidity
For each plant I give the ideal temperature. The second important factor is the ratio between heat and humidity: the higher the temperature the greater the humidity must be. Plants will tolerate summer heat rising to 26–32°C/80–90°F only if there is commensurately an increase in humidity levels. At this time for many of the plants that were used to steamy conditions in their native tropical habitat, trays of damp pebbles become doubly essential. Conservatory rooms should be kept as humid as possible, because the greater area of glass causes temperatures to rise quickly. Good air circulation is important too.

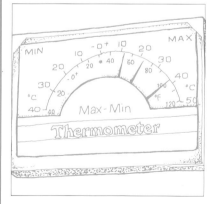

Winter also brings problems for plants. There are draught-hating species and those that wilt with temperature fluctuations – such as when heating systems are turned off during the middle of the day. Whilst temperatures can acceptably be 2–4°C/5–10°F lower during the night than the day, there are danger spots where plants will suffer more.

Measuring temperature
To know precisely what is going on you need a maximum/minimum thermometer which will accurately give you the fluctuation in heat. These are widely available and record differentials over a given period. They are useful for plants that are particularly sensitive to temperature fluctuation, such as *Gardenia* or *Stephanotis*, and for delicate plants in judging, for example, the differences between being in a position at ground level or higher up on a shelf. Temperatures do vary more than you imagine in a relatively small growing area.

The effect of temperature extremes
* Flowering may not occur in species used to different conditions in their native habitat, and that is why in this book I have tried to give as much idea of native circumstances as room permits. If certain plants are used to low or high temperatures for a season and you are unable to give similar conditions then growth will be stunted.
* The plant may wilt despite the compost feeling moist; always try to control temperature changes over a number of *days* rather than hours if the plants are to survive in a healthy condition.
* Growth may die back in extremes of temperature, and a great many of the plants in this book will not survive frost.

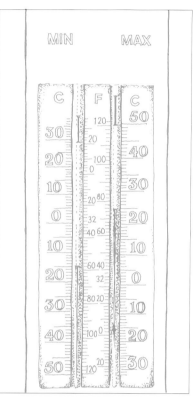

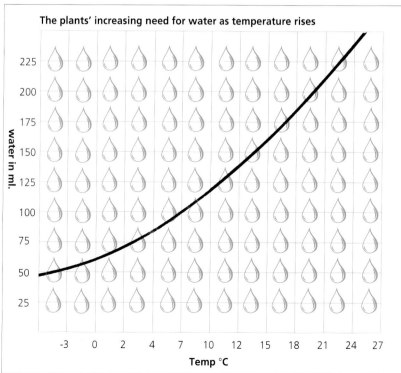

The plants' increasing need for water as temperature rises

water in ml.

Temp °C

Most rooms have different climate areas. It is important to consider these when siting your plants

Doors can be a source of draughts

Windows: if open, draughts may be a problem, but if the window area faces the sun for any length of time it may become very hot

Air-conditioning units may be a source of cold draughts which will harm sensitive leaves

Televisions, fridges, cookers can be sources of intermittent hot air which may or may not suit different house plants. In order to avoid hot draughts many plants would be better sited on a shelf above in order to deflect the full blast

Radiators: hot, dry air can be harmful to many plants

Repotting and potting on

What is repotting?
There is a great deal of confusion between *repotting* – literally removing a plant from its pot and repotting it in the same container, perhaps with fresh soil – and *potting on* – moving a plant into a larger sized pot. The most important reason to repot or pot on is when a plant shows signs of distress: repotting rejuvenates, potting on allows further development.

The time to repot/pot on
* When plants are potbound and have no room to grow larger root systems.
* When the leaves discolour from lack of nutrients taken from the soil, which has become exhausted.
* When the plant outgrows the pot – this happens frequently in certain plants during the early part of the growing period.

The optimum time to pot on is when the growth season is commencing – for most plants in early spring – so that the new growth has room to develop properly. Never repot unless you have to during the dormant period.

Repotting
Remove the pot. Gently discard about 4cm/1½in soil from the surface of the compost, taking care not to expose the roots. Prune the roots if the plant is really potbound. This should only be done in drastic cases or to encourage new growth where roots are blackened and decaying, but plants need very special care to survive the experience. Ensure good drainage and repot the plant using fresh compost to top dress it to its original level. Indoor plant fertilizer can be incorporated into the dressing.

Pots
Clay, terracotta and plastic ones are commonly available. Each has advantages and disadvantages. Terracotta and clay look more natural than plastic, and hence suit some plants better than others. Plastic ones are 'unbreakable', although they do split on occasion: they come in a range of different colours – browny red, green, black and cream are commonly seen.

Pots are normally round and as wide as they are deep (i.e. the diameter = the depth). There are square pots too, and half-pots, useful for shallow-rooted plants.

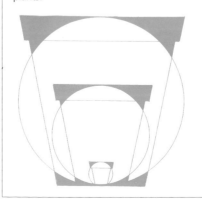

The potting on process

1 Begin by immersing the plant in a bucket of tepid rain water for an hour to give it a thorough soaking. Remove any moss that has grown on the surface of the soil.

2 Choose an appropriately sized new pot, ideally just a little bigger than the previous one. (New, unglazed clay ones should be soaked in water until air bubbles cease to rise to the water's surface; this prevents them from absorbing the moisture intended for the plant.) Why shouldn't you choose a much bigger plant to avoid the messy repotting business and provide for years of future growth? Because the compost becomes sour with age, and, with the extra amount of compost not occupied by the roots, the plant stands a much higher chance of becoming waterlogged.

3 Set up the new pot with good drainage: a concave crock from an old broken pot to cover the hole in clay pots, and a shallow layer of pebbles over the many holes in plastic pots will suffice. Top this with a layer of appropriate compost, then place the plant on top. Fill the sides with more of the new compost. Pack it in firmly but gently. Air pockets should be forced out but the compost should not be so compact that water cannot penetrate it. Water the new compost thoroughly around the edges of the pot from the top, ensuring it drains well.

Removing the old pot
This can be difficult and exasperating. Turn the plant over and tap the base firmly. A sharp knife can be used to loosen the sides. In extreme cases you may have to push a blunt piece of wood up through the drainage holes or even break the pot.

Compost and potting mix

Compost is the source from which indoor plants can thrive and flourish. It comes in two different types — soil-based (loam) and soil-less (peat). Loam is good-quality soil which has been mixed with coarse sand and peat, together with additional plant foods.

Indoor plants do well in both but due to the variability of good loam most commercial nurseries use more peat-based composts.

Advantages of loam-based compost
* The weight of the potting mixture is able to support larger plants.
* It dries out more slowly than a peat-based compost.

Disadvantages of loam-based compost
* Not easy to gauge quality as the composition of the soil is uncertain. Always buy from a reputable supplier.

Advantages of peat-based compost
* Quality does not vary.
* It is lighter and easier to handle.

Disadvantages of peat-based compost
* It can be difficult to water once it has dried out.
* Due to its lightness there is little anchorage when potting on a large plant.

Exceptions
Orchids and cacti all need specially mixed composts, which are widely available at superstores and garden centres.

There are a range of composts readily available to meet your every need, but first read the instructions carefully to ensure that you have the right product.

Acidity/Alkalinity
Indoor (and indeed many garden) plants prefer a slightly acidic soil to an alkaline soil. The tell-tale sign of unsuitable soil is the leaves turning yellow (chlorosis, see glossary).

The term Hydrogen ion concentration (pH) is used to measure acidity/alkalinity in soil. The scale is from 0—14 with 7 being neutral. Soil-testing kits are readily available at garden centres. The band that indoor plants will tolerate on the pH scale is between 4.5 and 8, i.e. on the acidic side.

Composition of growing mediums

Nitrogen 1.5 per cent

Phosphorus 0.15 per cent

Potassium 1.5 per cent

Magnesium 0.2 per cent

Calcium 0.5 per cent

Sulphur 0.1 per cent

Iron 0.01 per cent

Zinc 0.002 per cent

Copper 0.0006 per cent

Manganese 0.005 per cent

Boron 0.002 per cent

Molybdenum 0.00001 per cent

All growing mediums require the above elements for healthy growth (see p. 236.) These elements, however, make up only 4 per cent of the total. The other 96 per cent is made up by oxygen, hydrogen and carbon.

Acknowledgements

There are a number of people I would like to thank for their work and help on this book.

First, thanks go to Jacqui Hurst for her lovely photographs and Sally Maltby for her beautiful watercolours and line drawings which illustrate the book.

A big thank you also to: Susan Haynes and Suellen Dainty for their research; Geoff Hayes for the design of the book; Mrs Peter Bowen, Alison Cathie and Paul Whitfield for opening up their homes to our photographer for the location sections at the front; Marks & Spencer PLC; Floreac, Belgium; Jan Kochem at Lemflora, Denmark; the Royal Horticultural Society, the Garden Centre Association and Chivers Flowers of London.

Finally, thanks to Kyle Cathie, Caroline Taggart and Beverley Cousins at Kyle Cathie Limited for their hard work, and to all those in my company whom I have pestered from time to time.

Photographs
Grateful acknowledgement is made for permission to reproduce the following photographs: Andrew Lawson, page 24; Boys Syndication, 12; Eisenbeiss, page 36; Flower Council of Holland, pages 35, 41, 61, 108, 132, 134, 150, 167, 179, 195; Hugh Palmer, pages 18, 19, 25; Mercurius UK Ltd, pages 57, 63, 82, 101, 102, 113, 119, 124, 135, 144, 155, 156, 157, 161, 167, 176, 177, 188, 211, 217, 221, 222; Photo Horticultural, pages 93, 210.